T0361443

THE ART OF LEADERSHIP
THROUGH PUBLIC RELATIONS

THE ART OF LEADERSHIP THROUGH PUBLIC RELATIONS

The Future of Effective Communication

BY

PATRIK SCHOBER
PRAM Consulting, Czech Republic

United Kingdom – North America – Japan
India – Malaysia – China

Emerald Publishing Limited
Howard House, Wagon Lane, Bingley BD16 1WA, UK

First edition 2023

Reprints and permissions service
Contact: permissions@emeraldinsight.com

British Library Cataloguing in Publication Data
A catalogue record for this book is available from the British Library

ISBN: 978-1-83753-633-7 (Print)
ISBN: 978-1-83753-630-6 (Online)
ISBN: 978-1-83753-632-0 (Epub)

INVESTOR IN PEOPLE

'To Francis Ingham, a true leader and advocate for the public relations industry. Your unwavering commitment to promoting ethical practices and professional standards will continue to inspire and guide us as we navigate the future of this dynamic field'.

TABLE OF CONTENTS

ABOUT THE AUTHOR

Patrik Schober, the current Managing Partner, started up PRAM Consulting agency in 2002. At that time, PRAM saw an opportunity to provide consultant services in the field of communication to large multinational firms that were entering the Czech market, not knowing the environment and customs. He was awarded as PR Personality in 2018 and with his team he has won several global and local PR awards, such as Sabre, European Excellence Awards, Golden Drum, ICCO Global Award, EFFIE and Lemur – Czech PR Awards.

Patrik graduated from International Relations at the University College Prague and completed internships at Holmes College in Sydney and the University of California Irvine. He began his career at publishing house Computer Press.

Patrik is also well known in his field as a Chairman of the group of independent PR agencies Worldcom through which he shares his observations with other world PR leaders. It enables him to share the guardianship of a client at an international field. At the same time, Patrik was a Chairman of the Board of Directors of Czech PR Association (APRA), which is a professional association whose primary mission is to present the field of public relations to both professionals and general public. Besides that, to promote best practice, set up ethical standards and start discussions among professionals and to promote the good reputation of the industry.

Patrik is passionate about passing by the knowledge of public relations practices. Besides devoting his time to lecturing at the University of Economics and the Charles University Prague he has been hosting his seminars called PR Brunch since 2015. During each seminar he and his guests introduce and discuss new trends in public relations industry. Beside that he advises companies how to gain so-called leadability through his workshops titled Leadership Lab that presents a unique facility providing training and coaching in all the facets of leadership behaviour.

Patrik and his wife live in Prague and they are proud parents of two teenage girls. When he is not working, you can find him running long-distance trails or climbing mountains.

FOREWORD

There could not be a more timely moment for this compilation of essays from some of the world's leading PR practitioners and commentators. I would urge anyone interested in the future of our profession to read them eagerly and in detail.

COVID has transformed PR. These terrible years for us all have radically changed the way our industry works; its profile as a professional service; and its prospects and composition.

When COVID struck, our industry like the rest of the world reacted with fear and trepidation, but also with resolve. As I write these words, all of the PRCA, ICCO and Provoke data that I see say that we are slightly bigger than we were a few years ago; that the industry is hiring at pace; and that it is buoyantly confident about the future. Which is a world away from how so many of us felt in 2019.

Against that context of a return to growth, it is an opposite moment to take stock of the nature of challenges ahead of us in the coming 20 years. And this book does just that.

To this end, I would make eight key observations.

1. *We know where the main areas of future growth can be found.* Not everything has changed. Many trends that had been apparent for years have simply been accelerated. So, for example, we know that the key fundamental drivers of growth in our industry have remained constant for over a decade.

    • Companies and CEOs in every region of the world are paying more attention with every passing year to corporate reputation. Something which we saw exacerbated during COVID, where companies' reputations and customer loyalty and engagement soared or crashed depending on the decisions they made.

- The blending of disciplines works in our favour, as organizations shift spend from expensive and often ineffectual advertising campaigns to us instead, based on our ability to narrate a story well.
- We continue to expand the range of services on offer, with a move away from simply pure, old-fashioned PR.
- And we own digital. (of which more below.)

Sectorally, there is remarkable consistency. For years now, the big three areas of growth have been IT and technology; healthcare; and financial and professional services. There is no reason to expect this to change.

2. *New professional tools need to be embraced constantly.*
Our industry's great strength is the speed with which it adapts to change. As Roger Hurni and Sarah Polak argue, our industry needs to embrace AI, apps, behavioural design and many other tools besides. Our industry knows of all of these tools, but over the coming years, it must embrace them more whole-heartedly. And over the coming decades, it must embrace whatever new tools, now unthought of, become available.

If we are honest, as an industry, we fail to invest adequately in the professional development of practitioners. In part, this is probably down to the old-fashioned view that in an industry with no real barriers to entry, skills can be picked up on the job. But if PR aspires to be a true profession, then that needs to change, and the coming years need to see the development of proper frameworks for organizations and individuals alike – a point made by Jürgen Gangoly when he writes about leadership and standards.

3. *Measurement and evaluation sophistication continue to increase, but far more needs to be done.*
If our industry is to continue to move up the professional services food chain, then it needs to embrace ever-more sophisticated proof of our value, as Richard Bagnall argues in his contribution.

Now we know that much progress has been made here.

- Awareness of, and use of, International Association for the Measurement and Evaluation of Communication (AMEC) tools has never been higher.
- While avess are alive still, their extinction continues around the world. They are almost completely dead in North America and the United Kingdom, for example.
- Clients are increasingly requesting more varied and detailed measurement methods, such as engagement and sentiment metrics.

But if we look forward to where the industry needs to be in 20 years, then it must surely commit to real investment in data-driven insight. Not just gut feel or exceptional writing, key as those two abilities will always be. But advice founded on rock-solid foundations of knowledge. That's the future. Because if we don't do this, then others – for example, lawyers and management consultants – will.

The tools to meet this goal exist now and grow more accomplished every year. We just need to pay for them – and yes, that involves clients and organizations allocating proper budgets here, not expecting post-campaign evaluation done for free or on the cheap.

4. *Digital and the embrace of technology and AI are the way of the future.*
There is an excellent ICCO video of Peter Chadlington from a decade ago giving this typically forthright advice: 'If your people can't do digital, then train them in it or fire them. Because otherwise, you won't have a business left to run'.

The good news here is that the most recent ICCO World Report tells us that three of the top four areas of agency investment are digital. That needs to continue, and I believe that it will do.

5. *Public expectations of purpose as well as profit are simply going to accelerate. This is an area where we can be critically important to colleagues and clients.*
Public expectations were already changing fundamentally pre-COVID. But COVID turned this sentiment into something

resembling the default position. Melissa Waggener Zorkin, Fred Cook and others talk about this. Our industry can guide brands to turn well-meaning words into reality, helping to address the societal challenges that people care about.

And in this regard, and as this book notes, we are missing a trick on ESG. We are uniquely placed to own this area in the same way that we own digital. It plays to all of our strengths and insights.

But an ESG strategy is meaningful only if it is measurable, deliverable and embraced wholeheartedly. Points which the Ethical Compliance Initiative in Washington DC and the Institute for Business Ethics in London have made strongly. And that's the truth speaking to power which our industry needs to offer.

6. *Talent is a critical threat to our future that must be addressed in the years ahead.*
As Alex Aiken and Rich Leigh point out, we need to make our industry a far more attractive place to join and continue in. For years now, industry data have shown us that recruiting and retaining talent is a fundamental problem for us. In fact, many industry leaders say that there is no greater challenge.

In essence, it's about a number of factors, all of them overlapping.

- The industry isn't diverse enough. And it needs to become so. Years of hard work have failed to make much discernible impact here. Far more needs to be done.
- The gender pay gap needs to be eliminated. Again, despite much effort, the picture barely shifts. And this needs to change too.
- Other professional services attract our people – the reverse is rarely true. And if we are honest, much of the reason for this is pay. I would relate this back to the need to prove value – if we could prove better the value that we deliver, then quite simply the industry would be larger, and able to pay people more, and retain more of them.
- And finally, the always-on culture. Exacerbated by COVID, and a major turn-off for many, particularly those with caring responsibilities, or wanting to maintain a decent life balance.

On the positive side, our experience of home working and remote working has shown that it is far from impossible to be effective without permanently being in the office. This may well help us to do two things: offer more flexible working patterns and so keep many of those who otherwise leave our industry; source talent regardless of physical location, but instead based on skills and attitude alone.

7. *As society's ethical expectations have evolved, so too have our industry's expectations of what is acceptable and what is not. But over the coming decades, the existing minority that eschews ethical practice needs to be diminished much further.*
We know from our data that while two-thirds of practitioners feel that their own industry is ethical, a third do not. Which is a pretty striking number. If so many of us don't believe that we ourselves and our colleagues have a moral compass, then how can clients and wider society trust us to represent them ethically?

Wide disparities of ethical expectations exist globally. And if we are honest, wide disparities of ethical enforcement by professional bodies exist globally too. But this situation cannot hold in the future because those public demands of purpose of ethicality are shifting all around the world, albeit from different starting points. A rising tides carries all boats as they say, and the same will surely be true of the PR industry and its attitude towards ethical behaviour over the coming decades.

8. *A final thought*
Having highlighted both the positives and the negatives that I see, I do think that it is important to end this foreword on a positive note. Because the industry that I recognize is a permanently positive one; adaptive to circumstances; and with a track record of growth in size, salience and importance that few if any other professional service sectors can match.

So, looking forward 20 years, I hope that we will see a PR community that is significantly larger even than the one we have today. More diverse. Even more structured. Even more respected. And I truly believe that we will see all of these things.

Francis Ingham
Director General, PRCA
Chief Executive, ICCO

Who is Francis Ingham

Francis Ingham had been in the professional communications industry for over 20 years. He studied Politics, Philosophy and Economics at Oxford University before starting his career as an advisor to the British Conservatives and the Confederation of British Industry. He was Director General of the Public Relations and Communications Association (PRCA), the largest and most dynamic professional body for PR and communications professionals in the world. For the past seven years he held the position of Chief Executive of the International Communications Consultancy Organisation (ICCO) which represents 41 national PR associations. Francis Ingham was committed to PR education at all levels – he was external examiner at the American University at Richmond and Visiting Lecturer at the University of Westminster. He appeared in both the UK and global selection of the best and most influential PR professionals – PR Week's PowerBook.

ACKNOWLEDGEMENTS

My biggest thanks go to my wife Lucie for her lifelong support and to my two daughters Kateřina and Tereza, because my world is a happier place with them in it. Peaceful family life gives me the space to pursue my business, work, sports and last but not least, it made this book possible. Without my family, I could not have accomplished half of what I have achieved in the last 20 years.

Over the years, I have been influenced by many people who have contributed to my career. I am grateful to them for sharing and giving me their time. This includes past and present colleagues at PRAM Consulting. Without them, the company would not be where it is now. The first, however, was my business partner Karel Kapinus. Even though our entrepreneurial paths diverged over time, without Karel I probably would never have started the business.

Another partner to whom I owe the current success of my company is my long-time mentor Crispin Manners. I met Crispin at the Worldcom PR Group, and he has passed on lot of his knowledge to me. Crispin can shape my ideas into tangible projects and guides me toward overall effectiveness. Thanks also go to Jakub Štefeček, who is pushing me further in the field of business management.

Over the years, I have been greatly influenced by people in the professional organizations I participate in, whether it is APRA, Worldcom PR Group, or ICCO. I am grateful to my fellow competitors who have elected me to be the chairman of the Public Relations Association. Worldcom and ICCO have given me a global perspective on communications and management and provide me with great inspiration for my projects. There are dozens of people, members of these organizations, whom I would like to thank for sharing their experience and friendship. All the futurologists who have contributed to this book I have met in these organizations. I hereby thank them for the time and inventiveness they have given to their contributions to this book. I would, however, single out two without whom the aforementioned organizations could not operate. These are their Executive Directors, who have been my closest collaborators during my APRA and Worldcom presidencies: Pavla Mudrochová and Todd Lynch.

Public relations is essentially the same anywhere in the world, you 'just' have to respect and acknowledge the cultural differences in each country. This general rule ceases to apply the moment you actually start working in a completely different region. Matt Kucharski showed me how to do PR in the United States when he allowed me to work in his agency for almost a month, for which I owe him a big thank you. This internship showed me how ahead of the curve PR, communications and management are in the United States compared to Europe.

Almost 10 years ago, professional journalist Ondřej Aust and I discovered that no platform or person in the Czech market focussed on trends in public relations. So together we invented a series of communications trends meetings for PR professionals and called it PR Brunch. The series of seminars became an iconic and award-winning brand that helped PRAM Consulting become one of the top five PR agency brands in our market. PR Brunch is also the foundation for Leadership Lab (leadershiplabnow.com), a series of leadership training sessions. Both activities served as the springboard for this book. Thank you, Ondřej, for our long-standing partnership!

I couldn't have written the book you are reading without Kateřina Matesová, with whom I put together most of the text. She has been giving me feedback on my ideas while editing the text into a friendly and readable form.

As we all know, we can be creative through activities where we relax and completely unwind. For me, such activities are various sports. While I clear my head when running in the city and often come up with interesting ideas (like how to tackle a current campaign brief), there are activities, especially extreme ones, that I cannot undertake alone. My friends may be in other fields, holding various management positions in global companies or running businesses, but they are always a great inspiration to me.

Thank you all very much for being with me!

INTRODUCTION

It's summer 2000 and I'm having lunch with my friend Thomas LaRocca. We are talking about what kind of business we could run because working for an IT literature publishing house is not very fulfilling.

We both have our degrees in international relations and communications, but we don't apply our knowledge to our jobs. We have travelled almost all over the world. We watch foreign companies coming to the Czech Republic that do not understand the Czech market. We have long conversations about marketing and distribution with them from the position of 'mere' employees of a publishing house, providing helpful, free advice. So, we decided to monetise our knowledge and skills. For we see that while foreign companies hire local managers responsible for product development and sales, they usually outsource marketing and public relations (PR) to external advisors and consultants, including PR agencies.

Thomas and I knew how PR agencies worked in the Czech market, and from our studies, we also know theoretically how they should work. Of course, our ideas at that time differed considerably from the later reality and are probably best summed up by the famous joke about a public relations manager who reads the newspaper in the morning and looks for articles about his clients, goes to lunch with a journalist at noon and in the afternoon figures out which client he will charge for lunch. So, we come to a clear conclusion: having a PR agency can't be that complicated! We agree to run the idea through our heads and come up with concrete steps at the next lunch.

Eventually, Thomas said, 'We don't know anything about PR', and backed out of the project. I didn't let such a small thing discourage me, and I started a PR agency with another colleague from the office, Karel Kapinus. Together we got the agency off the ground and for over a decade, until our paths diverged, our joint business worked well. We didn't join a giant global agency that would have shaped us in its image, but perhaps that's why our novel approach was successful with clients.

We saw a gap in the market, which was based on our reasoning with Thomas – helping global companies coming to the Czech Republic who don't know the Czech media market, journalists or the language. Aware of their limitations, they knew they needed a partner to create a communication strategy and campaigns to kick-start their business. So, that's what we did! In the beginning, our work focussed primarily on media relations. Over time, we realized we could deliver much more value and began to look at a wide range of tools and activities.

Twenty years are behind us. We have stayed abreast of changing audience expectations and use communication methods to elicit the desired action. We emphasise the uniqueness of our clients through their 'WHY', the reason and purpose of their business. We tell their story in the right way, to the right people.

Our vision has endured – giving international organizations the momentum they need to succeed in the Czech Republic. It works because we proactively communicate for our clients, even in moments when we need to protect them through crisis communication. We have won many prestigious local and international awards. We have become members of the Worldcom PR Group, the largest network of independent PR agencies in the world. This gives us access to global know-how. Together with our partners from around the world, we share our expertise in delivering immediate impact and lasting value to our clients. This is necessary because PR is constantly changing – especially consumer behaviour and the way the media works. And the pace of change is accelerating. But what will it take to lead that change?

What's in store for us in the next 20 years, and how can we be ready to capitalize on the changes to come? The answer to that question is the reason this book was written. After 20 years in PR, I see more than ever that every organization needs to be able to navigate the challenges they meet on the way to their destination. Leadership comes from being able to be prepared for the challenges to come, so you can select the most effective path to your destination.

That is why I have approached world PR figures to identify the communications transformations that we will all meet in the next 20 years. Their predictions, which you will read in nine thematic chapters, paint a picture of an industry that is facing dynamic developments, ethical and technological challenges, and above all, growing strategic influence. I then respond to the predictions with practical guidance on how to prepare for such a future. We delve into topics such as reputation, measuring campaign impact, brand activism, talent retention and the impact of artificial intelligence, which will be critical to success. In each chapter, I introduce important tools and processes that will help you not only meet the challenges of the future but even use them to your advantage. Last but not least, I try to summarize how to prepare for them in a way that will enable you to achieve leadership status.

Government and legislative changes, or crises such as the global COVID-19 pandemic, clearly demonstrate the need for a communications method that gives companies market and leadership momentum. Let's look together at what this means for the future of PR.

1

WHAT WILL AN AUTHENTIC COMMUNICATOR LOOK LIKE IN THE FUTURE?

Phases of Public Relations and Its Role in Leadership

Warren Bennis, an academic and pioneer of leadership studies, once said: 'Leadership is the ability to turn vision into reality'. This phrase, in my opinion, perfectly captures the importance that leaders have for the future of professions, organizations and entire nations. They are the ones who shape reality from their ideas and visions. They are the ones who make the strategic decisions that subsequently predetermine their visions to success or failure. They are the ones whose actions influence many aspects of our work and social lives. The attitudes, beliefs and performance of employees, the culture and communication climate of an organization, the perceptions of stakeholders – all of these are in the hands of leaders.

But let's go back to the beginning: communication as a tool for successful leaders. Of course, even the leaders of the future cannot do without public relations. The American writer James Humes, the author of President Eisenhower's speeches, famously said, 'The art of communication is the language of leadership'. This is illustrated by another president at another time, as Paul Holmes argues below.

* * * * *

PRESIDENT ZELENSKY SHOWED EVERYONE WHAT A LEADER LOOKS LIKE

Paul Holmes

In a nutshell, I could say that the authentic communicator of the future will look a lot like Ukrainian President Zelensky. Right now, as I write these lines, he is showing the world the power of communication in shaping the global agenda.

What makes him so effective? Qualities that all great leaders and great communicators will need in the future. The empathy that makes him understand the emotions, hopes and fears of others. The humility to put the interests of the people he leads ahead of his own personal agenda. Integrity that allows him to communicate honestly and openly, even when times are tough, and messages are difficult. And the courage to speak truth to power, even when doing so may be dangerous.

I would argue that it is courage that divides people into leaders and others – and it doesn't just apply to those who involuntarily find themselves in the middle of a war. Courage means doing things in accordance with your vision, even if it is risky. This is exactly what President Zelensky has shown. Many experts predicted a lightning defeat for his country. President Zelensky has shown them what can happen when a leader stands up for his convictions. As a former actor, he proved the truth of the statement that one is not born a leader but becomes one. All those who predicted his quick defeat had to admit their mistake.

I wish communicators in the field of public relations would show similar boldness when facing uncertainty, such as fears about what artificial intelligence will bring (and take) to the industry; worry about how to confront the pervasive pressure for sustainability; doubts about whether PR can attract and retain increasingly confident talents; dread about the breakneck pace of new social media and its content formats; and anxiety of accepting responsibility for what public relations brings to clients' desks. These are exactly the reasons why many PR professionals still cling to AVE metrics, why they still quantify media outputs and manage media relations in Excel spreadsheets, why the profession has low credibility with the public, and why the contribution of public relations is usually measured not through the lens of the actual value it offers to a company but by the enumeration of the effort expended.

I am convinced that there is uncertainty behind the scenes. Fear that our work may turn out to be worth less than we think.

In this respect, too, President Zelensky can be an inspiration. In the face of necessity, he has thrown away fears and shown all aspirants to the position of a leader how it is done. Let his story be an inspiration to PR professionals to overcome their own – and often unjustified – imposter syndrome and set out to make changes that will lead their organizations to better results and increase the strategic relevance of the entire industry. The future expects it.

* * * * *

> *Courage means doing things in accordance with your vision, even if it is risky.*

Who Is Paul Holmes

Paul Holmes has spent more than 30 years studying and analysing global public relations. In that time, he has built a reputation as one of the world's foremost experts on professional communications. He began his career working for a local newspaper in the north of England and he became news editor of  PR Week in 1985. In 1987, he moved to New York to launch the short-lived US edition of PR Week, and later joined Adweek. In 2000, he launched the Holmes Group, which provides news, research, analysis and insight on global PR. It also presents the SABRE Awards competition – the most

(Continued)

(*Continued*)
important PR awards in the world. The group's flagship title, PRovoke Media (p/k/a The Holmes Report), covers the public relations business in the Americas, EMEA and the Asia-Pacific region. In 2011, Paul Holmes was inducted into the International Communications Consultancy Organization (ICCO) Hall of Fame.

PR as a Discipline of Leaders

Given the above, it is not surprising that mastered communication, and therefore public relations, are among the most important tools of successful leaders. Leadership and communication go hand in hand, as we will see in the following paragraphs. Before we start, please note that these paragraphs contain my own opinion on past and contemporary public relations based on my experience and knowledge. However, I'm not a historian nor media theorist.

For a manager, the ability to communicate well is almost a moral imperative. After all, to be effective, a manager must be able to persuade, express responsibility, delegate work, create and manage a value system and provide support and motivation to his or her team. All this can be achieved through effective leadership, proper planning, monitoring and most importantly communication! In my opinion, effective and accurate communication is the most important among the factors mentioned. It is the manager's communication skills that motivate and inspire team members to work and achieve goals, whether within the team or the entire organization. The importance of communication is matched by the time it requires: According to one older study, a manager spends 70–90% of his or her time each day communicating with his or her teams and others in the workplace. Effective communication then means effective leadership. In other words, anyone who wants to go from being a 'mere' manager, director, or even a minister to a true leader cannot do without learning the ins and outs of good communication and public relations.

Even the Egyptian rulers understood this, which is why the discipline of PR is as old as civilization itself. Pharaohs built an image of divine beings among the people through their lieutenants who spread stories of their fantastic achievements, skills and qualities. Shamans and tribal chiefs passed on their wisdom and life experiences through stories told around fires. We could call it 'PR 1.0'. The dominant mode of communication was purely one-way, flowing from the ruling individual or group to the subjects. This modus operandi persisted until the dawn of twentieth century when Ivy Ledbetter Lee laid the foundation for modern PR as we know it.

Throughout the millenniums, public relations and its storytelling has persisted, but the fire around which we now figuratively sit and tell stories is modern technology. Change is also happening on the commissioning side and with an increase in communication channels and their capabilities. PR managers and communications professionals have a key role to play and their job is to tell a good enough story that engages and achieves its objective, i.e. to reach a key audience and make them change their minds or actions.

The 'PR 1.0' is followed by 'PR 2.0'. Its main hallmark is the interaction of two parties. It involves both the sender of the information and the recipient, who provides feedback. This 'two-way' phase of public relations is linked to the development of Web 2.0 and the initial online connection. This eventually evolved into communication on social networks, blogs, or discussion forums, where the target audience gets the floor and PR professionals encourage their feedback. The '2.0' version then transformed into the more advanced 'PR 3.0' in a short period of time. It was then that communication professionals became more aware of the possibilities of traditional and new media and started to use them for so-called integrated campaigns, combining different channels and types of communication.

> The fire around which we now figuratively sit and tell stories is modern technology.

PR 4.0

Therefore, the next evolutionary phase is 'PR 4.0'. The fourth generation itself usually represents something modern and progressive – Industry 4.0 or Web 4.0 are well-known examples. The phrase Public Relations 4.0 encompasses not only the attributes of advanced twenty-first century PR and its growing strategic importance to business but also the challenges facing this dynamic discipline, such as measurement, ethics, appropriate use of all available channels, and education. At the same time, the modern transformation of PR is also linked to contemporary technological trends – including digital transformation, artificial intelligence (AI), virtual and augmented reality, robotics and automation – which either directly affect the practice of the PR profession as a whole or are increasingly becoming the subject of emerging activities.

PR 4.0

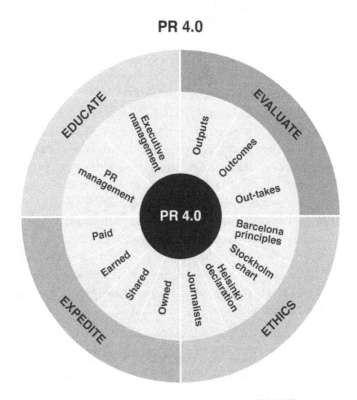

SOURCE: LeadershipLabNow.com

Working With Data

The first challenge PR professionals face is dealing with the amount of data they receive from different communication channels. To continuously improve communication campaigns, it is necessary to properly decode and use the extracted data, for example by using

AI technology. However, there is also a catch. Although the application of this technology in the communications industry may expand soon, the human input of a knowledgeable PR professional cannot be replaced. It's just going to be a little different than what we've been used to – more focused on aspects that machines can't do, like creative and intuitive activities or networking.

Media Relations

Another challenge for PR professionals nowadays is communication with journalists, or media content[1] creators, who can be virtually anyone thanks to modern technologies and online community platforms. PR specialists are thus faced with the question of how to establish and grasp cooperation with influencers or bloggers.

Professional Ethics and Education

A decisive point in modern PR is also the observance of professional ethics, whether it is the issue of fake news or the way individual spokespeople, PR agencies, or PR managers communicate. At the same time, the level of education is also related to the perception of ethics. The biggest challenge is the education of the whole market, not only of communicators but also of senior management. The completion of PR specialists' work – and the driving force for its continuation – is not a mere list of activities carried out, but a clear presentation of the impact public relations has on the client's company, which deepens mutual understanding and partnership cooperation.

All this matters in leadership for one simple reason: the importance of PR across companies and countries is growing. It is estimated that the value of the global PR market will increase by more than 46% between 2020 and 2025, to a value of nearly $130 billion.[2] Focusing on local businesses, Czech Public Relations

---

[1]Jirák, J. and Köpplová, B. (2015) *Masová média*. Portál. For purpose of this book, I accept the sociological view on media content as 'media messages that are transported as information from sender to receiver'.
[2]*Public relations (PR) market value worldwide in 2020, 2021, and 2025*. (March 2021) Statista.com.

Association's (APRA) annual survey of its members shows that 65% of CEOs take corporate reputation seriously, and roughly a similar number view branding and communications as a long-term issue. Up to 70% of them are willing to invest sufficient funds to cover the work of PR professionals – both external and internal – whose job it is to bring value to the company through communication campaigns.[3]

THE ESSENTIAL STEPS TO BECOME AN AUTHENTIC COMMUNICATOR OF THE FUTURE

1. *To be a leader, pay attention to communication.* The past and the present have taught us that the ability to communicate well is essential for a leader or a manager. The future will be no exception.

2. *Don't underestimate the growing strategic importance of PR to business.* The importance of PR to organisations will only increase, as will the value of the global PR market.

3. *Keep an eye on technology, for it will have a significant say in the future.* Digitalisation, artificial intelligence, virtual and augmented reality, robotics, or automation will have an impact on corporate leadership and the communications industry itself.

4. *Start with PR 4.0.* Public Relations 4.0 is the PR of the future: it encompasses the attributes of advanced twenty-first-century PR, the growing strategic importance of communications for business, and the challenges of contemporary PR, such as measurement, ethics, technology, new communication channels and formats, and the training of PR professionals.

5. *Define the challenges facing PR in the future.* The future will bring new realities to the PR profession; prepare for them early. The individual challenges and ways to meet them will be discussed in the following chapters of the book.

------

[3]APRA. (October 2022). *PR agencies' revenues and prices were on the rise in 2021. Due to rising costs, agencies will become more expensive.*

2

HOW WILL ORGANIZATIONS GAIN THE MOST CREDIBILITY IN THE FUTURE?

Reputation, Image and Personal Branding

The field of public relations has its basic principle encoded in its name. More than 100 years have passed since modern PR was established, and nothing has changed in this respect. Relations are still the pillar and core mission of our work: through clear communication, *we use PR to create relations not only with the public but with all stakeholders.* Because when others understand us (and we understand them), trust is built. And without communication, trust, and relations, there is no good reputation. It's almost safe to say that no matter how our world changes in next 100 years, building relations and trust will remain the purpose of public relations.

* * * * *

PEOPLE WANT BRANDS TO CREATE STABILITY IN THE WORLD

Melissa Waggener Zorkin

In 2022, I've seen a tremendous shift in how brands think about their reputation — in fact, nearly every brand we partner with is intensely focused on how they show up in the world. All around us, brands are making real-time decisions about how and where to engage. They know that the decision points are fast and frequent, and that the choices made now will be reflected in their legacy with decision-makers and the public at large.

It wasn't always this way — so what's changed? Our research at WE Communications shows **heightened expectations from the public and decision-makers for brands to create stability in a world rocked by climate change, social upheavals, and war.** To drive that stability, people want and expect brands to be brave and show up in ways they hadn't considered before. At the same time, people express scepticism about a brand's position they may view as inauthentic. So, it's essential that actions are always true to a brand's purpose.

There are also more factors that influence brand leaders on topics spanning race, human rights and inequality. Navigating those influences makes it critically important that leaders at every level deeply engage with a diverse group of stakeholders, prioritizing underrepresented groups like women and people of colour. And it's not enough to simply listen. Leaders must internalize what they hear so they can anticipate how their actions may impact their people, their customers, and other stakeholders.

The brands that thrive in the future will have learned to expertly balance disparate and even competing influences. They will do so by operating with a deep grounding in their purpose and will put people first — always. With consideration and bravery, they will take bold action. And they will tirelessly work to empower diverse voices to keep unlocking the ideas we need to create a more just, equitable, and sustainable world.

> The brands that thrive in the future will have learned to expertly balance disparate and even competing influences.

*****

Who Is Melissa Waggener Zorkin

Melissa Waggener Zorkin's name is primarily associated with her agency WE Communications, which she founded in 1983. Her dream was to tell (and create) stories about technology and innovation as she sensed that both would play a transformative role on the world stage. Over the decades, Melissa Waggener Zorkin has worked with some of the world's biggest, best known and most innovative brands, always focussing on the purpose, the 'why', that drives them. Together with her 'co-pilot' Pam Edstrom, this is how they built one of the largest global independent communications agencies in the world from scratch. WE Communications never loses sight of the human factor and PRWeek magazine named the agency one of the best places to work in 2020, 2021 and 2022. Melissa Waggener Zorkin is a big advocate and supporter of women and diversity in business. The significance of her work and unique leadership skills earned her place in the PRWeek Hall of Femme in 2017 and her induction to the International Communications Consultancy Organization (ICCO) PR Hall of Fame in 2020, and her induction into the PRWeek Hall of Fame in 2022.

Find Out How Stakeholders Perceive You

We want to step up our communication.

We need to get out of this reputation crisis.

We'd like to find out how stakeholders perceive us.

These are the most common requests we hear as PR professionals from the mouths of corporate executives. *Reputation* is indeed an increasingly important value in today's turbulent world. But the problem arises when companies are wondering what to do with their desire for 'the best reputation around' – and they don't know where to start. But one thing is certain. In the pursuit of a positive image, it is necessary to forget about short-term goals that can be mindlessly sprinted towards. Truly high-quality, and above all meaningful, reputation management resembles orienteering. You need to know where you are, where you want to get to and, most importantly, constantly check the direction you have set. Real leaders don't run fast, they run far.

> Truly high-quality, and above all meaningful, reputation management resembles orienteering. You need to know where you are, where you want to get to and, most importantly, constantly check the direction you have set. Real leaders don't run fast, they run far.

GET A REAL WORLD PICTURE OF YOUR REPUTATION

To launch truly targeted and effective communications, you need to know the baseline – what individual stakeholders think about the brand, how they feel about it, what media they consume, and what they want to hear (and in what form). As PR professionals we collectively refer to this in-depth diagnostic as reputation analysis. Unfortunately, this approach is still not standard in the PR environment. However, if companies want to take the lead, their leaders should not underestimate the need for preparation, i.e. a reputation analysis. It will show its worth many times along the way.

A reputation analysis consists of several areas that need to be examined and analysed. These are the media, specific stakeholders, and a power that is currently not to be missed – social networks.

For all these areas, you should not be satisfied with quantitative data alone, but also use qualitative methods of measurement. In the case of the media, this is not only monitoring media outputs (quantity) but also media analysis (quality). The latter can reveal how often – and, more importantly, in what way – the media cover your brand. It analyses the quality of the media, the tonality of the outputs, their genre and form (e.g. whether or not they contain photos and other visuals). The media analysis also includes a comparison with competitors and the resulting share of voice. It will also show which topics, in the context of your business, certain stakeholders pay attention to, how they talk about your brand and in which media they do so.

Now it's the stakeholders' turn. In their case, the survey method often works best. While this may sound old-worldly in the age of big data and machine learning, it's one of the most effective forms of gathering information from customers, shareholders, clients, and employees. In addition, here too, technology is making our job as PR professionals easier through online surveys that allow us to interview many people anonymously in a short period of time (which also makes them perfect for market research). You can also choose to meet in person, either in the form of an interview or a focus group. Whichever form of interviewing you choose, the objective should be to find out what the target groups are interested in and how they feel about the brand.

For brands that operate in the online world (which is the vast majority these days), social media analysis is also an indispensable part of reputation analysis. You should use specialized integrated or external tools (e.g. social listening apps) that can track brand mentions, user activity on company or other profiles, as well as overall customer sentiment and its evolution over the period under review. Such findings will then facilitate the creation of a communication strategy and help your brand shape its online communication, its language, tonality, and focus. In the future, reputation analysis will be used more and more to set strategy and achieve all the communication goals there are.

HOW TO SEGMENT STAKEHOLDERS

Returning to the terminology of orienteering, reputational analysis is a compass that helps you determine your current position and therefore the direction you need to take. The result of a reputation analysis is therefore to set out how to communicate to each stakeholder. To make your orientation in the results of the analyses easier, there is a very handy tool: the stakeholder matrix. In this matrix, you can rank all stakeholders according to their interest in information about your brand or company (horizontal axis) and their importance and influence (vertical axis). To give you an idea, in the 'Consult and engage' box you will probably find CEOs and customers, and in some cases, interested and engaged employees.

Let's demonstrate a practical application of the matrix on one of my clients. Preciosa Lighting is a world-class manufacturer of designer lighting. It has local production in the Czech Republic, local employees and customers all over the world. What does its matrix look like? The 'Consult and engage' section includes customers, i.e. reality investors, developers, interior designers and architects. The company organizes events, workshops and meetings to keep them engaged. In the 'Inform' box, we find the company's employees, who receive information about what is happening in the company (in which they have a high interest but lower influence), as well as the rest of the Preciosa group. In the 'Monitor' section we find other players in the market, including competitors. 'Keep satisfied' box is then particularly relevant for market regulators such as state and local government.

The resulting position of all stakeholders will greatly facilitate the preparation of the communication strategy. This is because you can better determine how much time and activity to invest in each group during the campaign. In addition, the different fields of the matrix determine the different communication strategies you develop based on the reputation analysis you have carried out. While nowadays companies often have one unified communication strategy, I expect that in the future, such communication strategy will be much more segmented and specifically targeted to individual stakeholders.

Mendelow's Power-Interest Matrix

Interest of Stakeholders

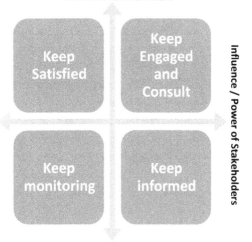

Adapted from: Mendelow, A. L. (1991) 'Environmental Scanning: The Impact of the Stakeholder Concept'. Proceedings From the Second International Conference on Information Systems 407-418. Cambridge, MA.

KNOW THE DIFFERENCE BETWEEN AN IMAGE AND A REPUTATION

How does image relate to reputation management? And is there any difference between the two? Many laypeople, as well as professional communicators, consider these terms to be interchangeable. Others differentiate them. Edmund Gray and John Balmer, for instance, describe image as something that can be created more quickly and easily than reputation.[1] According to them, corporate image is the mental picture of the company held by its audiences. I would add that the image of an organization often differs between different target groups or even between individuals. In contrast, reputation is much more strongly rooted in the consciousness of not only the wider public but also all stakeholders. This is because it is based on the organization's long-term performance and the setting of corporate values and purpose (we will discuss these topics in Chapter 6), which concern both

[1]Gray, E. R. and Balmer, J. M. T. (1998) 'Managing Corporate Image and Corporate Reputation,' *Long Range Planning*, 31(5), pp. 695–702. Available at: https://doi.org/10.1016/s0024-6301(98)00074-0.

external and internal stakeholders. Reputation is thus a kind of social capital of the organization, which, unlike image, has a more lasting value and greater resilience to temporary influences. As Gray and Balmer write: 'A favourable reputation (. . .) requires more than just an effective communication effort; it requires a meritorious identity that can only be moulded through consistent performance, usually over many years. A co-ordinated communication programme can, however, reinforce and promote a positive reputation'. This is why building a favourable reputation is one of the main tasks of PR.

As Melissa Waggener Zorkin rightly points out, it is essential that a brand always takes steps that are in line with its real direction. It is the consistency between image and reputation that creates brand credibility. And without credibility, there is no leadership. The bridge that connects the two should be the real actions and decisions that companies make every day. PR is there to help with these decisions, basing them on expertise and relevant data.

* * * * *

WE NEED TO BUILD HUMAN NETWORKS AS THE FOUNDATION FOR LEADERSHIP

Matt Kucharski

For organizations to establish themselves as the most trusted in the future, they will need to have strategies that blend what has been successful in the past with the recognition that stakeholder attitudes have evolved – in terms of who they trust, where they get their information and their willingness to listen to points of view that are different from their current beliefs.

Within this environment, nearly every leading organization strives to transform. The ones that transform in a way that doesn't just benefit them, but also benefits the majority of their stakeholders, will be the ones that ultimately earn the strongest levels of trust.

That trust will come from two fundamental elements – ACTION and INTERACTION. It starts with action. Organizations that transform need to start by actually making the decisions and initiating actions against them. I like to call it 'burning a calorie.' Those actions alone, though are not enough. Organizations can only be successful if their stakeholders ALSO take action – by starting something, stopping something, continuing something or permitting the organization to do something. That requires interaction – communications that seeks to build awareness, understanding, appreciation, and action.

In the future, the organizations with the most robust, resilient human networks will be the ones that build the most trust. It's not unlike building the same thing in IT. A robust and resilient network has nodes (the people), connections between those nodes (the communications channels), data and protocols that run across the network (messaging and storytelling) and monitoring (measurement and optimization). Competition in the future will not be organization vs. organization. Instead, it will be network vs. network. We're seeing that today in the private sector and between governments and economies.

And with artificial intelligence and machine learning, we will have more tools and technologies than ever before to build, use, monitor, measure and optimise those networks – aggregating structured and unstructured data that gives a fuller picture of the health of an organization's human network and its impact on business success.

* * * * *

> *In the future, the organizations with the most robust, resilient human networks will be the ones that build the most trust.*

Who Is Matt Kucharski

Matt Kucharski has been a member of the Padilla team since 1989 and its president since 2017. He holds degrees in journalism and business administration from the University of Wisconsin-River Falls. He has been an adjunct instructor of marketing and strategic communications at the University of Minnesota since 2001 and is a frequent panelist, guest speaker and moderator on a variety of strategic communications, marketing and business strategy topics. Matt Kucharski served as global chair of Worldcom Public Relations Group, the world's largest organization of independent communications agencies. He is also a member of the Arthur W. Page Society 'Page Up' programme and an accredited member of the Public Relations Society of America.

LEADERS ARE FACES OF THEIR ORGANIZATIONS

Strong bonds, quality relations, trust. No organization can really do without them. In the comparison to human interactions as networks, which Matt Kucharski aptly used in his prediction, I would like to dwell on the most important points that determine how strong and resilient a given network is – the individual nodes, i.e. the people.

For an organization to be strong, its leaders need to be strong. This is doubly so for trust. You have to start with yourself, by creating your own personal connections and networks.

How to achieve this? Introverts will be relieved to know that it doesn't matter how many conferences (and subsequent networking sessions) you've attended or how many business cards you've handed out. Here again, the most effective approach is a thoughtful campaign that improves the ability of corporate executives to interact, communicate, share and then evaluate their actions. So-called personal branding can yield much. Through professional personal communication between managers or key figures in an organization, trust in the whole organization can be strengthened. This was confirmed in a global survey conducted by Lewis PR in 2019 among 17,000 CEOs, 75% of whom confirmed that they consider active communication to be a key personal asset that has an impact on their career success. In addition, 91% of CEOs believe that companies where senior management actively uses social media as a communication channel are more trustworthy. The specific benefits of personal branding can be summarized in 10 points.

REASONS FOR PERSONAL BRANDING

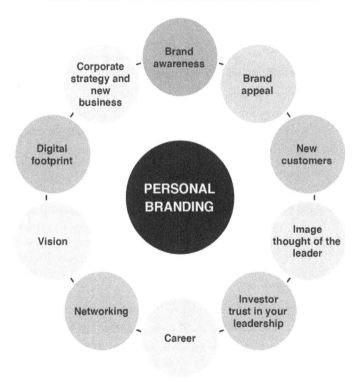

SOURCE: LeadershipLabNow.com

10 REASONS TO START PERSONAL BRANDING

1. *To increase brand appeal*

Once a company is publicly represented by a specific person, the brand becomes more attractive and trustworthy to customers. This is because customers can better identify with your company through the persona of its leader.

2. *To attract new customers*

The long-term communication of the leader of the organization to the target group eventually brings new customers.

3. *To strengthen the leader's position*

By speaking at conferences, communicating in the media, and focussing on professional topics, a leader can become a recognized expert in his or her field.

4. *To strengthen investor trust in your leadership*

Trust is a currency. This is relevant not only among customers but also among investors. A positive public attitude towards a company's management is a guarantee for current investors and an attraction for potential ones.

5. *To encourages career*

A successfully built image can not only influence a leader's position in the organization where he or she currently works, but also his or her possible future career in another workplace.

6. *To facilitate networking*

Attending conferences, being active in industry organizations, and proactively managing social media profiles open up opportunities for networking and building new (plus maintaining existing) contacts.

7. *To explain your vision*

Most leaders have a vision related to the organization they work for or the industry as a whole. Their own communication will give them the opportunity to explain the vision to all stakeholders.

8. *To improve the digital footprint*

The digital information about the organization and its leader must be both consistent with each other and consistent with corporate communications. In addition, a positive digital footprint of the corporate personality will support their other media relations. Journalists like to know something about the people they are interviewing in advance.

9. *To support corporate strategy and new business development*

By communicating in line with the corporate communications strategy, the CEO is also supporting corporate objectives.

10. *To improve brand awareness*

By linking all activities and taking a proactive approach to communication, the brand awareness of your company or organization will automatically increase.

The purpose of personal branding is to create a distinctive and visible personality that represents the company in line with the corporate communication strategy. The ultimate goal of these two interrelated communication levels is to strengthen the positive reputation and trust of all stakeholders. As it is true today that people buy from people (i.e. companies with strong and visible leaders), this trend will become even more significant in the future.

BUILDING A LEADER'S BRAND

There are three steps to create a functioning brand for your company's CEO/owner/founder. The first step is a personal branding workshop where personal goals and unique values are defined. In the second phase, create a plan of activities to support the personal brand. This includes building a website, blog or thought leadership programme, setting up social media accounts, and preparing a schedule of activities.

THE ACTION OF ACTIVISM

How proactive is **your CEO** in
speaking out about societal issues?

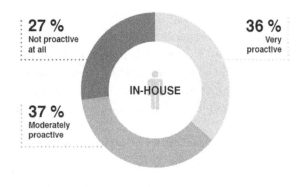

27 %
Not proactive
at all

36 %
Very
proactive

IN-HOUSE

37 %
Moderately
proactive

How proactive is **your agency's CEO**
in speaking out about societal issues?

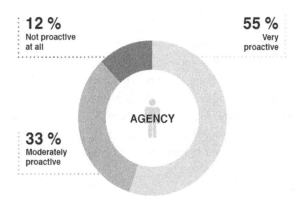

12 %
Not proactive
at all

55 %
Very
proactive

AGENCY

33 %
Moderately
proactive

SOURCE: 2022 Global Communication Report,
USC Annenberg Center for Public Relations

The third step is to focus on reputation management itself. This includes author and bylined articles, interviews in selected media outlets, managing social media profiles, or securing participation in industry organizations or conferences.

We must not forget that media relations alone – which many people mistakenly think of as synonymous with PR – is not enough to communicate and build a leader's brand. If you want to achieve the desired effect and goals, it is crucial to involve many other disciplines, including digital communication, marketing, analytical tools, and business strategy. It follows that brand building for CEOs or business owners must be handled by senior staff in companies or agencies who can manage the sub-activities and link them into one integrated campaign. This is the only way to achieve truly professional personal communication of managers or key figures of the organization, which will contribute to the creation of an image of a leader in their field, explain the company's vision and, last but not least, strengthen trust in the company's leadership – or strengthen the human network that Matt Kucharski talks about.

Finally, I will return to Melissa Waggener Zorkin's prediction from the beginning of this chapter. The future will bring many changes to organizations, their networks, and individual leaders. One of the most significant will be society's growing expectations for leaders to be active on society-wide issues, Melissa Waggener Zorkin suggests. I agree and add: This requirement will place even greater demands on leaders and their teams. Indeed, activism can be a very explosive discipline. Without the know-how of communications and PR professionals, leaders risk dropping out of the public debate in the future or – and this is the worse option – harming the company and themselves through their performance in this debate.

THE ESSENTIAL STEPS TO LEAD THROUGH CREDIBILITY

1. *Maintain consistency between what you do and what you say.* This is the only way to gain the trust of stakeholders.

2. *Find out what your stakeholders think of you.* To be a leader, you need to know where you stand with your stakeholders. It is therefore worth investing in a reputation analysis and using the results to plan your communications to each stakeholder group.

3. *Try new ways of reputation management.* Continue to cultivate activities that have worked well in the past to promote and maintain reputation. But don't forget about new trends and tools such as social media and community building. Keeping your finger on the pulse of the digital age will pay off.

4. *Crisis can come at any time, be prepared for it.* In an era of increasingly polarized society, the lightning effect of the share button, and the ubiquitous fake news, it would be unwise to think that crisis communications don't concern you. Conduct an internal reputation crisis preparedness audit, develop a crisis plan and virtually test how the plan works. Your business may thank you one day.

5. *Don't underestimate personal branding and human networks.* There is no strong organization without strong leaders. A strong leader brand will have a positive impact on the credibility of the entire company.

3

IS JOURNALISM THE NEXT
BIG THING?

Ethical Principles of Public Relations and Journalism

Would PR exist without journalists? The answer (currently) is no. Although public relations cannot be fully equated with media relations, the media and journalists play a very important role in our industry. According to the Paid, Earned, Shared and Owned (PESO) Model™ (we will discuss this communication model in detail in Chapter 4), journalists influence at least a quarter of the work of a PR professional. The gradual decline of traditional journalism is thus deeply affecting PR. It is in our best interest that the media are well and healthy and that journalists are not only our partners, but above all guardians of democracy, freedom of expression and the quality of media content.

However, this is becoming increasingly difficult. Journalism is ceasing to be a prestigious discipline that once attracted thousands of students. Journalists are no longer the sole purveyors of information; they have been replaced by more or less important celebrities, influencers and basically anyone with a social media reach – and unfortunately often zero understanding of what journalism is, how to work with sources or what ethical principles there are. This, of course, has a negative impact on the media scene and its standards. Fewer graduates mean less competition, yet there is increasing pressure for performance and quantity. Gone are the days when every journalist was dedicated to 'his/her' topic. The speed of information is more important than its context; the picture is more important than understanding it.

Can the current dismal situation be reversed? Juan Señor believes that there is a way to preserve the meaning and quality of journalism. But it lies in the very foundations of journalism, such as the desire to find and tell the truth – values that neither influencers nor PR specialists can replace.

* * * * *

BEWARE OF THE NEXT BIG SHINY THING

Juan Señor

*We have been here before and we will be there again in 20, 30 or 100 years – technology will not save journalism, **only journalism will save journalism.***

The digital revolution has transformed the news business as the invention of the Gutenberg printing press did half a century before. But transformation is not salvation.

While the means and scope of distribution have changed the media landscape forever – the core business of journalism remains the same and more important than ever before.

Artificial intelligence, the metaverse and inventive social media formats are often touted as being decisive for news if the profession wants to survive. They are the next big shiny thing that may 'save' journalism from a long-predicted extinction. But we have been here before: virtual reality was supposed to change and transform journalism – it did not (the goggles never reached mass appeal). Twitter and User Generated Content was supposed to displace news platforms – they have not. Tablets were supposed to kill print – they did not. And the list goes on.

The problem is that many believe technology is the message – a new medium that inexorably displaces and dispels the old as it emerges.

When it comes to social media, if your media is good, it will become social. It always has and it always will.

Technological breakthroughs are brilliant and welcome to improve and expand a message – a story. But that story still needs to be reported, contrasted, written, edited and produced. No amount of AI, or what may follow, can replace the human process of reporting, editing and creating an original story.

The Panglossian view of technology as a transformative force for good just because it is invented is naive. This view often distracts from the need to invest and protect the core business that is journalism. Rather than investing in human talent, in newsroom staff and training – executives misguidedly buy the latest Silicon Valley narrative of transformation and disregard the core business.

In 20 years, we may consume journalism in inventive ways through bedazzling devices that are physical, metaphysical, or ethereal. But the journalism will still have to pass the same human test of acceptance – is it new, is it informative or entertaining, is it provocative, is it moving, is it accurate, is it objective and independent, is it documented with indisputable facts, does it speak truth to power, does it give a voice to the voiceless, does it publish something that someone does not want published?

As we say at INNOVATION Media Consulting: 'Journalism is good business and if it is not good business, it is not good journalism'.

No matter how much technology we throw at, apply to or filter our journalism through in the coming 20 years, if we cannot get the journalism right humanly, technology will not save us.

Only journalism will save journalism.

* * * * *

No amount of AI, or what may follow, can replace the human process of reporting, editing and creating an original story.

Who Is Juan Señor

Barcelona native Juan Señor is the President of INNOVA-TION Media Consulting Group in London, one of the world's leading news media consultancies. The list of his experience is truly impressive. He worked for seven years as a war and conflict reporter for PBS's NewsHour, and has also served as London correspondent of International Herald Tribune Television then owned by The New York Times and The Washington Post. His work has been nominated for an Emmy Award and his TV show Media Report was voted Europe's Best Business programme. He is also a former Visiting Fellow at the University of Oxford. Juan Señor is a sought-after keynote speaker, moderator and commentator on the media industry and is quoted frequently in leading publications such as *The Economist* and *The Financial Times*. When not devoting to the media business, he campaigns disabilities via means of fundraising expeditions to the ends of the earth. He is conversant in six languages.

WHO WILL BUY EXPENSIVE NEWS?

Widening the gap in society is likely to divide those who are wealthier, better educated and therefore informed, and those who are economically weaker, making them potential recipients of disinformation. One reason for such a future scenario is the changing business model of independent media, which will be forced to raise their prices and abandon the free content model in the fight for survival. This is what Juan Señor suggests in his prediction: only good journalism will be good business, and if anyone wants to indulge in such journalism, they will have to pay for it. For this reason, we can expect a dramatic increase in the price of quality media content. While the educated and economically more powerful segments of the population will be able to afford this quality and independent content, poorer citizens will not. They will thus become the ideal target group for the partisan media agenda and tabloid media as well as conspiracy websites. This process will be further amplified by social media bubbles, which manage to sustain the 'always free' model through massive advertising. It will be inside these bubbles where divisions in society will further accelerate.

The result will be a society divided not only by an ever wider but also by a deeper divide. And it is the professional communicators who will find themselves in the front line. Their role will be clear and important: to actively prevent the spread of disinformation, to promote quality journalism, to disseminate only verified and truthful news, and to understand the needs and wishes of both of these groups (or many other groups) in society.

For only understanding can stop this gap from expanding. This will make PR experts indispensable for future leaders. Their task will be to work with a polarized society, to know the ethical standards of communication, to be able to follow them, to convince management of the need to follow these rules, to be able to navigate perfectly in the media environment and to deliver the organization's communication to all types of stakeholders.

For public relations, polarization of society poses a future challenge not only in terms of its day-to-day operations, communication with stakeholders and the creation of campaigns (we will discuss this topic more in Chapter 6), but also in terms of ethical principles.

POLARIZATION AND THE FUTURE ROLE OF OWNED MEDIA

ICCO conducts an annual survey on the usability of different media channels within the PESO Model™ (see Chapter 4). It shows that the share of owned media has been increasing over the long term. Of course, owned media bring many advantages to companies – it lets them have 100% control over the content and the audience to which this content is 'tailored'. Therefore, it can be assumed that public relations will also focus on communication within this channel in the future. But how will this affect the ethics of our industry?

Let's put this trend in the context of the University of Southern California's (USC) global survey. It shows that partisan media are seen as a major contributor to the polarization of society. Of course, it is not true that all partisan media contributes to polarization, but it can be said that every partisan media is owned. It should be added that the survey is influenced by the North Atlantic (and especially American) liberal media system, in which commercial private media predominate and the role of public media is traditionally weak. Nevertheless, even in the north and central European context, the research is very interesting as the strong influence of politically owned media has been penetrating this region in recent years.

In third place in the USC survey is social media, another popular PR channel. Here the indispensability of the journalistic craft in terms of ethical principles, working with sources, striving for balance and objectivity is shown. Companies do not have to follow any such rules in their owned media and social media accounts. They don't have to attach a competitor's opinion to each of their articles. Instead, they can publish incomplete or biased versions of the truth, promote their own political or technological agenda, and contribute to further polarization of society.

Why should a company that produces diesel engines report on the high efficiency of electric engines, which is close to 90%, while an internal combustion engine is barely a third as efficient? Conversely, why should a manufacturer of battery-powered electric vehicles communicate the negative environmental impact of its business in countries where fossil fuel electricity consumption predominates? Why should the two hypothetical companies inform anyone about new advances in fuel cell technology?

The bias of companies due to the nature of their business is a fact that we cannot change. It is therefore the job of PR professionals in owned media to stand in for the journalists, explain the ethical principles, and see that the organizations adhere to them. The way forward, as in the case of journalism, is quality content based on uncorrupted facts.

REASONS FOR THE POLARISATION
OF SOCIETY

Which do you think contribute the most
to the current level of polarization?

1 Partisan media outlets

2 Politicians

3 Social media platforms

4 Political strategists

5 Extremist organisations

6 Social media influencers

7 Activist groups

SOURCE: **2022 Global Communication Report,
USC Annenberg Center for Public Relations**

TO JOURNALISM BE A GOOD BUSINESS, PR NEEDS TO BE ETHICAL

Many will question whether it is possible for PR professionals to be the guardians of ethics and journalistic standards. The reason is obvious: Public relations does not have a spotless reputation in the eyes of the public. Our field is a bit like the proverbial cobbler's children. PR professionals face ethical challenges in their work every day – in fact, some companies feel that if the saying 'the end justifies the means' applies anywhere, it is in PR. The industry's controversial reputation is then no surprise. However, it is certainly true that those who want to become a true leader should not slacken in their moral demands on their business.

In the search for what is right and acceptable, industry organizations such as the International Communications Consultancy

Organization (ICCO) are here to help. Forty-one organizations from 81 countries around the world subscribe to ICCO's code of ethics, making a total of around 3,000 PR agencies. Two documents in particular are binding in the area of ethics. The first is the 2003 Stockholm Charter, which sets out principles in a wide range of areas – from objectivity and confidentiality to representing competing interests – to create a comprehensive ethical framework. It was complemented in 2017 by the so-called Helsinki Declaration, which commits PR agencies to the following 10 principles.

Helsinki Declaration

1. To work ethically and in accordance with applicable laws;

2. To observe the highest professional standards in the practice of public relations and communications;

3. To respect the truth, dealing honestly and transparently with employees, colleagues, clients, the media, government and the public;

4. To protect the privacy rights of clients, organizations, and individuals by safeguarding confidential information;

5. To be mindful of their duty to uphold the reputation of the industry;

6. To be forthcoming about sponsors of causes and interests and never engage in misleading practices such as 'astroturfing';

7. To be aware of the power of social media, and use it responsibly;

8. To never engage in the creation of or knowingly circulate fake news;

9. To adhere to their Association's Code of Conduct, be mindful of the Codes of Conduct of other countries, and show professional respect at all times;

10. To take care that their professional duties are conducted without causing offence on the grounds of gender, ethnicity, origin, religion, disability or any other form of discrimination.

Of course, these general formulations help to determine the ethical playing field of our industry, but in day-to-day operations, a PR professional must make decisions in the face of specific situations: Can I give the journalist a gift? How big a gift is permissible? What about an invitation to lunch? Is this client assignment consistent with ethics? Official ethical principles will never think of all potential situations, and the changing social and media landscape presents new challenges that the PR professional faces almost daily. Thus, behaving ethically can be much harder than it seems. One of the reasons is the ethical grey zone into which some clients– often unknowingly – push PR consultants. They'll want to 'just balance opinions a bit' but won't ask for astroturfing. They'll want to create a fake petition but won't utter the term front groups.[1] Hence, PR professionals need strong internal ethical boundaries. They must be prepared to face situations that cannot be rehearsed in advance.

Another important challenge will be the dissemination of disinformation, or rather its elimination. Technological breakthroughs that help journalism (such as artificial intelligence) can also lead it astray (for example, through deepfakes). Again, industry organizations could help. For example, the Czech Public Relations Association APRA (which is also a member of ICCO) has developed the following seven principles to combat disinformation.

APRA's Seven Principles for Tackling Disinformation

1. *Define.* Get clear on what disinformation is, how to identify it, where it most often comes from.

2. *Explain.* Use your media expertise to educate those around you about what disinformation is and what risks it poses.

3. *Do not advertise on disinformation sites.* This is a reputational risk to your organization and encourages the spread of disinformation. Support reputable media, you need them to do your job.

---

[1]Kaclová, M. (2022). 'Personal integrity of the PR professional as the biggest future challenge of strategic communication' [Charles University].

4. *Don't inform disinformers.* The operators and editors of disinformation media are not partners for a PR professional.

5. *Prepare.* Disinformation can threaten an organization's reputation and is a significant source for crisis communications. Define procedures for crisis communications that arise from disinformation.

6. *Refute.* Ignoring disinformation may not be the solution. When reputational threats occur, carefully consider how to refute disinformation to avoid reinforcing it.

7. *Verify.* Find independent sources of objective information, verify the facts with them, and engage them in communications when appropriate. Use fact-checking platforms.

The future role of public relations will indeed be crucial to maintaining a healthy communications environment. Aspiring leaders should therefore not underestimate the importance of investing in PR and working with communications experts to increase trust and confidence in their leadership. This will ensure that their message reaches the right stakeholders effectively, reliably and, above all, ethically. Leadership also comes with responsibility. Further, albeit unintended, polarization would harm everyone.

THE ESSENTIAL STEPS TO PREPARE FOR THE NEXT BIG THING

1. *Recognise that 'technology is not news'.* Journalism did not go bankrupt after the advent of cinema, radio, television, tablets, virtual reality, or social media. It won't go bankrupt in the next 20 years, and it will survive the polarization of society.

2. *Prepare for the media to change its business model.* Only then will journalism remain a good business and a partner for PR professionals.

3. *Dig deeper into your pockets for quality news in the future.* Prepare to find it expensive to buy a printed newspaper every day or read reputable media on the internet. Only a portion of stakeholders will be able to afford this investment. If you want

to communicate to the others, you will need to use different communication channels and probably a different way and type of message than you have been used to.

4. *Learn to work with an increasingly polarized society.* Communicating to the divided groups of society, navigating the changing media landscape, and ultimately communicating effectively to all types of stakeholders – this is what will make PR experts indispensable to future leaders.

5. *Invest in owned media.* Owned media will become increasingly important to organizations and leaders will make their owned media trusted by meeting key journalistic standards. PR experts should guard the ethics of their content and distribution. Only then will owned media not contribute to further polarization of society.

4

HOW DO YOU ENSURE THAT YOU USE THE MOST EFFECTIVE COMMUNICATION CHANNELS TO ACHIEVE LEADERSHIP?

Storytelling, Media Channels and The PESO MODEL™ Communication Model

Few industries rely on the power of stories as much as public relations. After all, have you heard of a leader – business or political – who doesn't have a powerful, or at least compelling, story to tell? Storytelling is a proven way to establish a strong bond with your target audience or to strengthen an existing connection. As a form of emotional branding, it influences how customers perceive your brand, how they identify with it, and whether they are therefore willing to purchase your products or services.

Storytelling has therefore been the essence of public relations since its inception. Bringing stories to life (and to public), together with the subsequent identification of the impact, aka measurement of the effectiveness of such storytelling – will only become more sophisticated in the future.

* * * * *

HOW TO ENSURE YOUR STORYTELLING REACHES THE NEXT GENERATION?

Stefan Pollack

Achieving leadership in storytelling, lies in how well the audience is understood and whether the story can illuminate, inform, clarify, enlighten, influence, encourage the audience – always keying into the traits, characteristics and values of the audience to whom the story is told. It needs to be cleverly crafted towards the goal of triggering desired action, be it in purchasing, direction taken, supporting a cause, or building or contributing to a trend.

Recognizing that the next generation, the oldest of which are just now entering the workforce, is unlike any other generation that came before them, it is important to speak their 'language'. They will expect civil discourse to connect on a human level and redefine what matters, how it matters, and to whom it matters, to broaden their perspective.

These are digital natives for whom diversity and inclusion are the norm. Stories need to be built upon with that premise in mind. Communication professionals with the greatest in-depth understanding of these expectations, those who can relate to this generation, and who can adapt to their need for human interaction skills and desires for immersive experiences, will emerge as leaders. As younger audiences celebrate the sight-and-sound technology that eclipses their stare-at-the-wall museum experiences, immersive experiences will dominate.

Unsurprisingly, an important channel for communicating with this next generation, is using devices – digital life – occupying more than their offline interactions. For example, the phone truly has become an extension of the person and the platforms and apps within it. Gen Z relies heavily on digital channels for communication, as should the storytelling professionals in our industry.

Nevertheless, it's interesting to note that Gen Z also appreciates face-to-face communication. It's the most effective way of communicating. As such, communicating stories via events, panel formats, symposiums, etc. will be another avenue to reach Gen Zers.

This generation will increasingly feel a collective responsibility for people and brands working together on environmental and societal improvements for a better, healthier world. Of note, Gen Zers' tend to see truth and morality as relative and can value authenticity so highly that they have an aversion to a lack of transparency and credibility.

Leadership is achieved when the stories you tell resonate and the desired results trigger action. It can be achieved with a deep understanding of the power of the stories we tell. Soft skills or 'human skills' as I prefer to call them – have never been more relevant, or more necessary.

* * * * *

Gen Z relies heavily on digital channels for communication, as should the storytelling professionals in our industry.

Who Is Stefan Pollack

Stefan Pollack is president of The Pollack Group, an integrated public relations and marketing firm with offices in Los Angeles and New York. For 30 years, he has managed clients in many sectors, from consumer products and professional services to technology and non-profits. He has served as president of the Public Relations Society of America, Los Angeles Chapter, and as chair of the Americas Region Board for The Worldcom Public Relations Group (Worldcom), a global partnership of independent public relations firms. He is currently the global marketing chair for Worldcom. Since 2001, he has taught as an

(*Continued*)

(*Continued*)

adjunct professor at USC Annenberg. He is the author of Disrupted, From Gen Y to iGen: Communicating with the Next Generation and is a member of the Forbes Agency Council, where he is often quoted and writes on the topics of social media, PR, marketing, and communications. In 2019, Pollack and his agency established the Noemi Pollack Scholarship at USC's Center for Public Relations, which annually awards a partial tuition scholarship to an undergraduate student pursuing a major or minor in public relations.

STORYTELLING IS THE WAY TO YOUR CUSTOMER'S HEART (AND BRAIN)

From the moment we come into the world, we are surrounded by stories. They are an integral part of everything we do – they accompany us at family dinners or on road trips, we see them on TV when we watch the news, we exchange them during visits with friends. It is the exchange of stories that has been our basic instinct since the Stone Age, when human communication was based on oral tradition. Even though millennia have passed and we now live in an age of 'instant gratification', interesting stories still resonate with us and appeal to our emotions and hidden desires. There are countless studies that conclude that the human brain responds better to stories than to hard data and bare facts. In fact, a good story activates the parts of the brain[1] that allow the listener to relate the story to themselves and their experiences, ideas or emotions, thus better engraving it in their subconscious and strengthening the connection with the brand.

It is the identification, creation and delivery of a compelling and recognizable story that aims to captivate customers – both existing and new – and bring them a unique experience that is at the heart of storytelling. Successful storytelling can encourage customer loyalty

---

[1]Wallentin, M. et al. (2011) 'Amygdala and heart rate variability responses from listening to emotionally intense parts of a story', *NeuroImage*, 58(3), pp. 963–973. Available at: https://doi.org/10.1016/j.neuroimage.2011.06.077.

and brand affection, and ultimately even increase company revenue, as the success of a company and its leadership position depends on brand perception.

HOW TO DEVELOP A STORYTELLING CAMPAIGN

How do you build and deliver a good story that gets under the skin of your target audience? A proven method for developing a storytelling project is the five-step cycle shown below. It includes the interrelated processes of devising, refining, implementing and evaluating any campaign.

STORYTELLING COMMUNICATION PROJECT DEVELOPMENT CYCLE

RESEARCH	GAINING INSIGHTS	CONTENT CREATION
– brand evaluation – market and target audience research – platform and social media analysis	– strategic planning – the creative part of the campaign – message development	– marketing materials – content for traditional and social media

EVALUATION	COVERAGE
– marketing analysis – market and business trends – campaign evaluation	– consistent storytelling across channels and platforms – media communications

source: LeadershipLabNow.com

1. *Research*

Research is the most important stage of campaign planning. Based on the objectives that the campaign should achieve, take a look onto the organization or brand itself, its competitors and the market environment. Focus on the campaigns that have taken place across all competitors, and also how the brand is perceived on social media. Don't forget to look at all the little details – from the founder's persona to the buying process. All the findings can then lead to adjustments or specifications of the campaign objectives and help you find opportunities for leadership.

2. *Gaining insight*

Once you have done your homework, i.e. you know everything about the brand and its segment, look for the blanks that will become the imaginary pitch for your campaign. Ask where you can generate more media coverage, which social networks are right for you/the organization, which posts will affect the target audience, or which stories haven't been told yet. These insights play a key role in following strategic planning, campaign creative and content creation.

3. *Content creation*

After all-encompassing research, and a search for gaps in the market, prepare content, which can take many forms: from a press release, video, article to an ebook. Everything must be ready before the campaign is launched, including the graphics. Regardless of the form, the content needs be attractive to the target group. We will take a closer look at specific aspects of creating a compelling story in a few paragraphs.

4. *Coverage*

Once you have the content ready, launch the communication and execute the communication strategy. Communicate on all the communication channels at your disposal – not only traditional and social, but also paid, earned, shared and owned media (the segmentation of media channels will be discussed in more detail in PESO MODEL™ section later in this chapter).

5. *Evaluation*

Evaluation is an integral part of the campaign. Ask whether it met our expectations, what went well and what needs to be improved next time (the approaches to measuring and evaluating a campaign are discussed in detail in Chapter 5).

At first glance it may seem that a storytelling campaign is a closed process, but this is not the case. Rather, as the graphic above suggests, it is a cycle and a long-term evolution, with evaluation followed by research again. Its objectives focus on the changes that the campaign has caused. These changes will then naturally result in the next phase of the cycle.

INGREDIENTS OF A COMPELLING STORY THAT INSPIRES PEOPLE TO TAKE THE RIGHT ACTION

For a campaign to have the desired effect and achieve its goals, its content must be easily digestible and delivered in a variety of forms to naturally stimulate the target audience through all the desired channels. The building block of such a campaign is a good story, which should meet the following criteria:

It's attention grabbing

A short and punchy story resonates more than a long-winded narrative with a vague message. Let's also remember that everyone today anxiously considers where to invest their time. You need to engage the audience quickly and keep them hooked on your content long enough to hear the whole story.

It has natural appeal to the target audience

The appeal of the story comes from what the target audience is interested in. Attractiveness also comes from whether the story is told in the customer's language. A good story helps them understand what your brand needs to tell them.

There is a hero

The hero is the one who uses the product or service. He or she may be an experienced user or just becoming familiar with the product as part of the story.

It leads to a measurable action

The story leads to a measurable action, e.g. completing a website registration, signing up for a newsletter or ordering a product. Evaluating a campaign based on measurable outcomes is part of the overall evaluation. In the future, no one will approve a communications campaign budget if we as PR professionals argue just for great media coverage. The driver will always be the measurable impact on the brand or organization.

It is visually interesting

Visual elements – photos, illustrations, gifs or videos – add dynamics to the story. Plain text doesn't excite anyone much. The reader responds to structure and visuals, as they are often just browsing and only engage when something catches their eye.

It is emotional

Allow your target audience to identify with your brand based on complex human emotions. From their list of emotions, you need to choose the ones that align with your brand identity.

It is creative

It tells a new story or tells an old story in a new way. It surprizes, delights, disarms, astonishes, shocks.

It speaks to the target audience through different communication channels

A thoughtful storytelling campaign delivers a story to its target audience through every possible channels – from traditional media to social, from flyers to e-books.

INGREDIENTS OF A COMPELLING STORY

DATA-DRIVEN STORYTELLING – THE NEXT BIG THING

Of course, storytelling is also affected by the changes that communication is undergoing with the advent of new technologies and mass data collection. The discipline that uses these tools is called data-driven storytelling. It aims to model stories tailored to specific audiences. No more crystal ball divination or gut feeling – data-driven storytelling, as the name implies, is based on the clever use of available data. This data can take the form of any information you can use in communication. This includes data about your organization, your competitors, the market, the socio-demographic profile of your customers, customer behaviour/journey and so on. More about capturing data will be in Chapter 8.

Data-driven storytelling is created by analysing and filtering large data sets to extract insights and uncover new ways of understanding information. They are tailored to the specific audience and context in which they are consumed. Data-driven storytelling simply allows us to convey information or point of view in the most effective way, with minimal cognitive load. By 'speaking the language of the tribe' it has a positive impact on the mental energy the audience must expend to understand our message, and ultimately how well that message will be received.

Why is data-driven storytelling so important? Why is it essential to know what your target audience is doing online and offline? To find the answers, we need to understand the barriers to reaching customers:

1. People are overwhelmed by media and content overload.

2. Marketing messages, mobile devices and other content are attacking consumers' attention on a daily basis. Multitasking has become the new norm.

3. People don't have enough attention. Consumers' brains are not expandable and can only absorb so much information at a time, in a way that still makes sense.

4. Consuming content requires tunnel vision. Consumers only focus on content that is relevant to them in the moment and filter out everything else.

5. The consumer journey is unpredictable. Consumers process content without a specific routine. Their purchase decision-making process is unpredictable, which greatly reduces the ability of brands to reach them.

As Stefan Pollack writes in his forecast, it is necessary to consider the changing habits of the emerging Generation Z, which is already a significant consumer group. As true PR professionals we cannot rely on mere impressions, or even our own children, nieces, nephews or siblings, to properly understand what content Gen Zers consume, in what media, in what ways, what gadgets they use, what they believe and what they hate, who they listen to and who they ignore. Generation Z is the most diverse generation yet to come into the world. On the one hand, it is the generation of activist Greta Thunberg. On the other, it's the generation of TikTok and one of the world's highest-paid models, Kendal Jenner. It is data-driven storytelling that will help us discover who to tell, what to tell and how to tell it to achieve the right impact.

WHO SHOULD YOU REACH FIRST TO GAIN THE GREATEST ADVANTAGE

How do you identify the right audience? The first question you should ask yourself is, 'Who should we reach first to gain the greatest advantage?' This is where the 1:9:90 model will help you. Use it to divide your audience into several groups and then create a targeted marketing or communication campaign for each of them. The model divides the audience according to average percentage into *influencers* (1% of people – despite the common perception that 'everyone is an influencer these days'), *listeners* (9% of people) and the rest of the market (90% of consumers). Influencers create original content, shape the market and set the tone and direction of the debate. This role has historically been provided by the traditional media. Today, this includes journalists and analysts, but also entrepreneurs, bloggers and, in short, almost anyone with a large audience and therefore influence. Another 9% of people, the so-called listeners, give content from influencers' context and reach.

They recommend, share, register, download, comment and let their community know what they think. The other 90% make up the majority of the market. They wait and learn. They consume content and decide how persuasively and credibly influencers and listeners tell brand stories.

For this reason, identifying who your influencers and listeners are and targeting these groups is an important first step, which enables you to affect the remaining 90%. This model is extremely useful as it will help you understand the principle of social media and how to engage with it in a campaign. At the same time, you will also ensure that the resources, effort and budget spent contribute to the best possible results.

The moment you have identified your audience and divided it according to the 1:9:90 model, it's time for listening, i.e. identifying and analysing the conversations of the target groups (influencers and listeners). As part of this analysis, you gather information about certain topics, how the audience views them, what media channels they use to do so, as well as the reactions of specific listeners. Then use the collected data to better target the audience.

Spotify is a great example. The streaming service collects data on what songs, artists and playlists its hundreds of millions users listen to. It uses the data it collects to suggest new music to each of these users based on their individual interests. In addition, it creates original content for its Spotify Insights blog based on the data. Another notable example of how Spotify uses data to tell stories is Spotify Wrapped. At the end of the year, the music app creates a unique presentation for each of its users that summarizes their music listening over the past 12 months.

Data-driven storytelling provides us with an editorial and creative framework to reach the right audience with the right stories. The data that this process yields is valuable. You can use it to create more stories, track the behaviours and conversations of your target audience, mobilize influencers, and continuously learn what content is interesting to your audience. Building a social media management manual is also an integral part of the process, ensuring that all content published, and how you communicate, is aligned with your brand purpose.

The beauty of data-driven storytelling is not in capturing the complete market, but in specifying the audience that is important to you. Based on what that audience is, where they are, and what they're interested in, you then target that audience – whether it's members of Generation Z, millennials or baby boomers – with precisely tailored content with impact that can be tracked and continually refined. This is the only way to make sure you're truly using the most effective channels to achieve your leadership goals, and many others.

Use PESO MODEL™ to Prioritize Where and How You Communicate

The PESO Model™ serves PR professionals very well in segmenting the media channels available to us when creating communication campaigns. This communication model was created by Gini Dietrich, founder of the successful platform (and book) Spin Sucks, in 2014. The name PESO Model™ is an abbreviation of the initial letters of the available media types, i.e. Paid (e.g. advertising or banners), Earned (i.e. the result of media relations), Shared (shared content, social networks, bloggers, influencers), Owned (e.g. blog, newsletter or magazine). PESO MODEL™ allows you to better understand the channels you are investing in and also helps you set the right measurable objectives, which are the basic parameters of successful PR communication.

Paid media allows us to distribute content in communication channels in the form of advertising, which gives us full control over the distribution of content and its message. Another advantage is scalability, reliability and speed of delivery. Specific examples are sponsored Facebook posts, advertorials, Google AdWords or newspaper ads.

Earned media is the opposite of paid media – it allows us to spread content without having to invest in advertising. The condition is that it must be interesting enough for journalists, bloggers and influencers to use it in their media. Moreover, if you can deliver attractive content on a steady basis, it will reflect positively on our

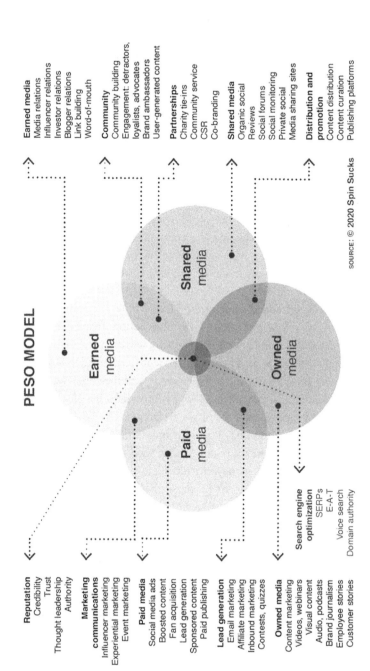

PESO MODEL

Earned media

Shared media

Owned media

Paid media

Reputation
Credibility
Trust
Thought leadership
Authority

Marketing
communications
Influencer marketing
Experiential marketing
Event marketing

Paid media
Social media ads
Boosted content
Fan acquisition
Lead generation
Sponsored content
Paid publishing

Lead generation
Email marketing
Affiliate marketing
Inbound marketing
Contests, quizzes

Owned media
Content marketing
Videos, webinars
Visual content
Audio, podcasts
Brand journalism
Employee stories
Customer stories

Search engine
optimization
SERPs
E-A-T
Voice search
Domain authority

Earned media
Media relations
Influencer relations
Investor relations
Blogger relations
Link building
Word-of-mouth

Community
Community building
Engagement: detractors,
loyalists, advocates
Brand ambassadors
User-generated content

Partnerships
Charity tie-ins
Community service
CSR
Co-branding

Shared media
Organic social
Reviews
Social forums
Social monitoring
Private social
Media sharing sites

Distribution and
promotion
Content distribution
Content curation
Publishing platforms

SOURCE: © 2020 Spin Sucks

media image. Influencers can also be used in shared media or 'invited' into your owned media.

The key player in *shared media* is our own audience, who spread our content by sharing or commenting on it. The resulting effect is amplified if you link the channel to earned media, typically through an influencer who places our content on their social networks. However, for shared media to work in your favour, you need to monitor it carefully and evaluate any conversations that relate to you and respond appropriately.

Owned media are channels that you own. That is, everything you create and publish on your blog, website, internal magazine or newsletter, whether it's employee stories, webinars, reviews or expert articles. In doing so, you continually strive to grow your audience and connect with other channels. In fact, what you place in your own media can usually be disseminated on earned, paid or shared ones.

The greatest added value of the PESO Model™ communication model is its effectiveness in content distribution and the measurement capabilities of a given campaign (we will discuss measurement in detail in Chapter 5). In creating content for the PESO Model™, start with one idea, the initiating moment, and then use it across all the communication channels at your disposal. So the idea remains the same, but the form of the message changes. The efficiency lies in the fact that you don't have to come up with several campaigns at once – you just come up with one that works across all channels. This saves time and money. At the same time, effectiveness also means the impact of the campaign on the organization running it. The target audience from different communication channels is consuming the same content, so you multiply the chances of it being perceived. Some sources (such as well-known marketing 'Rule of 7') state that we have to reach a target group up to seven times before they 'see' the message shared and it prompts them to take an action: click, buy, share an email, sign up for an event, send their CV, etc. PESO Model™ helps us with this. At the same time, paid, earned and shared media can act as traffic sources for owned media where you can convert (purchase, register, etc.).

How PESO Model™ Affects Media Relations

Storytelling and the PESO Model™ are also related to the direction media relations are taking. Data-driven content will make journalists' and influencers' jobs easier. Moreover, earned media collaboration is no longer the only alternative. The media landscape is enriched by emerging blogs and social media profiles, both shared and owned. We as PR specialists can invite professional journalists or influencers to collaborate on social networks or in advertising campaigns, use their own blog, and pay for advertorials in the media. This creates a much more connected media environment: We can turn a journalist who is also an influencer into the editor-in-chief of our corporate media, or nominate them to the board of an association we have created as part of public affairs.

Implementing the PESO Model™ into media operations can thus be one of the answers to the media crisis we discussed in the previous chapter. Like PR professionals, editorial boards and journalists will have to modify their messages for the different PESO Model™ channels in the future. Media outlets that are prepared to work with owned media organizations and fully exploit the potential of paid, earned and shared channels will be much better prepared for the challenges of the future and are more likely to maintain their importance, relevance and business potential.

One thing is certain. Media relationships as we have known them for generations are becoming a thing of the past. However, media relations is gaining much more importance as a result and can have a huge impact on an organization and its leadership.

THE ESSENTIAL STEPS TO ACHIEVE LEADERSHIP THROUGH THE MOST EFFECTIVE COMMUNICATION CHANNELS

1. *Don't forget digital channels when communicating.* Storytelling of the future cannot do without them.
2. *Use data to shape and target your story.* To determine who to tell, what to tell and how to tell it, utilize data-driven

storytelling. It will help you to overcome barriers, reach your target audience and achieve the right impact.

3. *Identify your influencers and audiences.* The 1:9:90 model is extremely useful as it helps you understand the principle of social media and how to incorporate it into your communications campaign. Once you have your influencers and listeners, the other 90% will follow.

4. *Segment your media channels according to the PESO Model™.* The PESO Model™ will help you navigate the channels available to you when creating communication campaigns.

5. *Create one campaign and capitalize on it across all channels.* The added value of the PESO Model™ is its efficiency. You don't need to come up with multiple campaigns, just one that works across all media channels.

5

HOW WILL YOU ENSURE EVERY CENT YOU SPEND TURNS INTO A LEADERSHIP DOLLAR?

Measuring Campaign Results, Generating Leads and Evaluating the Impact of PR

Numbers surround us. We can't do without ratings – in choosing a movie, a restaurant in a foreign city, and of course in public relations. Measuring the impact of PR has undergone a huge evolution over the past decade. No longer do we evaluate the success of campaigns by the number of media outputs or the number of journalists at a press conference. From the plethora of numbers that surround us, we choose the ones that help us discover the true impact of campaigns on the organization. The question of what the trends in PR measurement are is therefore absolutely crucial to the future of our work. Indeed, what we count, how and why has a significant impact on our understanding of the value of communication and its price.

* * * * *

JUST BECAUSE YOU CAN COUNT IT DOESN'T MEAN THAT IT MATTERS

Richard Bagnall

PR is not alone in feeling the heightened pressure of business. The 24/7 business environment, disrupted media, escalating crises, and increasingly tight deadlines have seen pressure mount across the many facets of critical work that we do. There's always more work to do with less time and fewer resources. Simultaneously, a heightened focus on accountability and proving return on investment has left comms teams trying to do as much as possible, with as little as possible, whilst delivering the biggest organisational value.

We all know that a busy comms team doesn't necessarily equate to a successful one. Ironically, 'busyness' leaves less time for the things that could potentially make us more efficient: planning, prioritising and aligning our activities with business priorities. The value we build is about the outcomes we achieve, not just the activity that often overloads us.

The promise of Artificial Intelligence (AI), and blind faith in the tools that ping out the magic answers, has left many comms teams even busier but less informed. AI can do the heavy lifting for us, but it takes data analysis and critical thinking to really draw a line between activity and outcomes. One of the incredible things, thinking back over the past 20 years and projecting into the next twenty, is that as much as things change, the fundamentals truly remain the same. There is a golden rule in the evaluation of communication: just because you can count it doesn't mean that it matters. **We have always known that counting what is easy to count— the big numbers—the discredited AVE, likes, shares, tweets, volumes, impressions can just make us ever-busier fools.**

AI should, and will, impact every area of our working lives. But what will really ensure every cent you spend turns into a leadership dollar is critical thinking. Planning, being led by data, taking each organisation's unique position in the world into account. And the tools are there to help us. Not just shiny dashboards but frameworks and well-trodden processes for thinking through what really makes an impact and how to declutter our working life to prioritise that. AMEC produces many free educational resources and I'd expect to see use of the AMEC framework become even more universal in the global comms profession.

Organisations that can truly unlock the power of data, and PR professionals that can make sure their efforts are accurately represented, will succeed. Lean into those helping hands, work with experts in communications measurement, be a value creator and not a cost centre. It needs to start and end with organisational priorities. The evolved practitioner who can clearly demonstrate their strategic effectiveness will be well placed to thrive.

> *We have always known that counting what is easy to count – the big numbers – the discredited AVE, likes, shares, tweets, volumes, impressions can just make us ever-busier fools.*

* * * * *

Who Is Richard Bagnall

It would be hard to find a greater expert on public relations measurement than Richard Bagnall, current co-managing partner of CARMA International and Chairman of AMEC, the International Association for Measurement and Evaluation of Communication. He has been in the PR and communications industry for more than a quarter of a century and has worked on the communications of some of the biggest global brands. He has also built and led some of the world's leading communications measurement consultancies, including Metrica, Gorkana and PRIME Research. He is a longstanding active member of the UK Government Communications Service's Cabinet Office Evaluation Council. He was inducted into the PR

(Continued)

(*Continued*)
News' Measurement Hall of Fame in 2017 for his lifelong
commitment to demonstrating and educating that communication has measurable value to organizations.

MEASURE TO EARN MORE MONEY

You need to measure. Constantly. I am certain that almost all PR
professionals agree on this statement. Despite this, there is an
entrenched notion in the communications industry that measuring
communication, and the effectiveness of our work, is extremely
difficult. We are constantly trying to find that magic wand that we
wave and our merits suddenly materialize in charts that we can finally
show to our colleagues, our board of directors or our parents, who
have always wanted us to be a doctor rather than a PR specialist. But
the problem is that there is no such magic wand – and we don't even
need one. In fact, there is already a plethora of tools on the market that
can be used to measure communication. But the magic is not to be
found in the tools themselves. The real magic lies in correctly determining what we need to measure, i.e. determining the kind of effectiveness that is needed. Choosing the right tool for measuring
communication comes down to answering the following questions:

– How do we communicate in a way that supports our (clients')/
  business strategy?

– What KPIs (Key Performance Indicators) are set?

– What activities are we going to undertake?

– How will the budget, context and planned activities affect the result?

COMMUNICATION CAMPAIGN MEASUREMENT CYCLE

Look at the diagram of the campaign measurement cycle below. It
clearly shows that you need to measure from the very beginning of the
campaign until the end. First, it is necessary to know the real objectives
of the organization. What do you want to achieve with the campaign,
what is to be changed? Do you want to gain leads, reduce employee

turnover, improve reputation? Based on these criteria, you should set your communication goals. If you have data from previous campaigns, you have a big advantage, because you can easily set ambitious but achievable KPIs for both areas. Once the organization's objectives are aligned with the communication objectives, the planning of the campaign itself comes next: conducting research, monitoring, creating a SWOT analysis and other activities. At the end, you have enough data to define a specific communication strategy.

But even then, you are not done with measurement, on the contrary. During the campaign, you need to measure its performance and compare the interim results with the set objectives and make changes to the approach if needed. Once the campaign is over, then comes another essential step: evaluating the results, especially assessing the impact of the campaign on the organization.

COMMUNICATION CAMPAIGN MEASUREMENT CYCLE

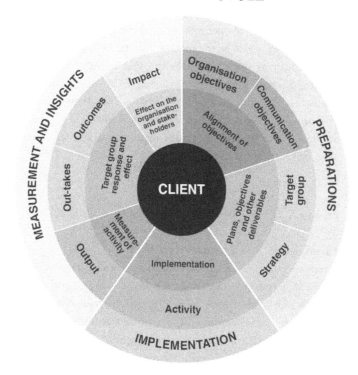

SOURCE: AMEC

SETTING THE RIGHT GOALS FOR THE CAMPAIGN

Imagine your goal is to have a specific topic accepted by the media. Setting such a goal will then allow you to identify qualitative and quantitative parameters to measure the effectiveness of how your message will be received in the media. If you set a specific goal at the outset, you can then easily see whether the desired change has taken place and the KPIs have been met.

If you are communicating through online channels or social media, answering the questions described above is even more important. For online and social there are dozens of different parameters to measure effectiveness such as bounce rate, likes, shares, engagement rate, etc. But the most important is whether your targets audiences have taken the right action as a result of your campaign. So, it's important to focus on what your client or your organization wants to create or achieve.

If you are trying to improve your organization's reputation, the best first step is to do a reputation analysis, i.e. define the start point. It is advisable to take into account the specific segments and target groups in which you can improve the organization's reputation as much as possible. However, you do not need to do a reputation analysis after every press release or any contact with stakeholders. It is recommended to conduct the analysis once or twice a year (we discuss reputation analysis in detail in Chapter 2).

So how do you achieve a functional campaign, its effective measurement and proper evaluation?

HOW TO ACHIEVE A SUCCESSFUL CAMPAIGN

1. *Communicate with internal stakeholders*

On average, up to five internal stakeholders make decisions about your campaign. Make responsibilities and expectations clear (e.g. through a project brief). Agree with your colleagues on the objectives, the planned results of the campaign and how to measure them. It is important that internal stakeholders stick to the agreed expectations and do not change them. That way, you will be able to make a good comparison after the campaign is over as to what your brief and inputs were and what results you achieved.

2. Dominate topics and channels

Reputation analysis will help you discover what topics to include in your communications, which stakeholders to target and what communication channels to use.

3. Use measurement tools

There are several sophisticated tools to help you measure the effectiveness of your PR. For example, AMEC has created an Integrated Evaluation Framework app that has been translated into 20 languages. This is the one Richard Bagnall mentions in his prediction. After adding all the inputs, objectives, activities and results (outputs, out-takes, outcomes) of a campaign, this tool generates a comprehensive one-page document that everyone can understand. A detailed description of the AMEC measurement tools and principles will be discussed in a few paragraphs below.

4. Measurement is not evaluation

From the beginning of the project, only plan activities that are measurable. At the same time, keep the end goal of the campaign and the integrity of the entire project in mind from launch to evaluation. You can use the data you capture to identify if you are on track or if changes need to be made.

5. Change the mindset

Ultimately, the success of a communications campaign is not a matter of the number of deliverables or the number of media mentions. Start thinking like your CEO who wants to see the impact of the campaign on sales, target audience behaviour change, lead numbers, reduced turnover, etc.

6. Don't be afraid of Smart Data

Media or social media monitoring is big data work. Learn how to combine this data with your organization's data such as the amount of sales, the number of job applicants, the number of calls to the customer service line, the number of leads aggregated on your website, etc. This will also make your communication meaningful in the eyes of your colleagues. Moreover, estimates show that using data to hone effectiveness will account for about 50% of a PR manager's work in the future.

TIPS ON HOW TO ACHIEVE A TRULY FUNCTIONAL CAMPAIGN

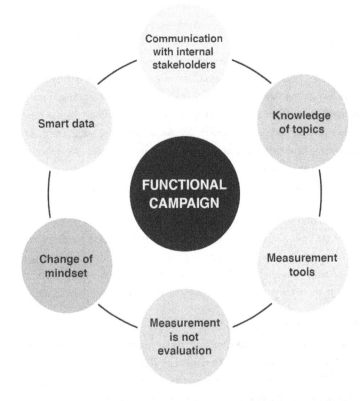

SOURCE: LeadershipLabNow.com

EVALUATE YOUR CAMPAIGNS AND ELIMINATE FOFO

Evaluation is undoubtedly the most important part of the campaign. It is by evaluating the impact of PR activities that you will gain arguments about the value of the PR department's work, which can convince company management, or decision makers, of the importance of investing in communication. Before we take a closer look at the evaluation methods that move your organization and its communications forward, I'd like to dwell on the popular, and reviled, measurement of effectiveness through AVE (Advertising Value Equivalency) aka converting editorial space to advertising value.

More than half of agencies around the world admit to still using AVE to measure PR value. This modus vivendi is overwhelmingly the result of client demands and corporate mechanisms. Besides the routine, the reluctance to abandon a well-known, albeit dubious, metric also stems from *fear of finding out* (FOFO). *Fear of finding out* describes a phenomenon in which people are reluctant to seek medical advice despite health problems because they are afraid to find out the truth about their condition. The term is widely used in many other fields, including PR.

In the words of a PR professional: What if it turns out we've been spending money on ineffective campaigns? What if the value of our communications is lower than we think? What if we find that our efforts have led in the wrong direction? The fear of the consequences such findings would bring to PR and marketing departments (or agencies) is too great and scary. Like patients refusing to see the doctor, some companies, agencies and their clients, prefer to turn a blind eye and carry on with their activities – sending out press releases, holding press conferences and keeping themselves blissfully ignorant. Because what if...

If you, too, have been diagnosed with FOFO, here are a few arguments why global PR experts consider AVE to be flawed and why to say goodbye to this metrics.

AVE IS NOT SUITABLE FOR MEASURING CAMPAIGN RESULTS BECAUSE

– It can't be applied to all media channels.

– It doesn't consider the target audience.

– It doesn't work with the quality of the outputs.

– Global PR experts consider AVE to be flawed.

– It confuses price with value. In addition, it works with list prices that are higher than the real purchase price of the advertisement.

Leaders across communications will move towards much more systematic and transparent campaign results measurement in the future. It's best to divide communications results into four categories:

Outputs

By outputs, we mean the sum of media outputs and their quality assessed against predefined criteria such as readership, reach, sentiment or quality. For example, ask what the reach of paid advertising was, how many visitors came to the website and what the media reach of the published articles was. In this category, you can also apply so-called media analysis, in which you examine media outputs over a certain period of time, often in comparison with competitors.

Out-takes

Out-takes provide a more sophisticated measurement of a campaign, where you look at the number of people who were reached by your activities, how your message was received by them, or the reasons why your campaign was ignored by the target group – i.e. different aspects of target group activation. Out-takes metrics include engagement, click-through rates, organic traffic, etc.

Outcomes

Outcomes refer to a comprehensive evaluation that is central to the decision-making of the company's top executives. Look for a change in the behaviour or opinion of the target group. You should be interested in the specific impact of the campaign on sales or how the target group's opinion of the brand or product has changed. In the case of a political campaign, you could count, for example, the outcome of an election among the outcomes.

Impact

The impact of a communication campaign is the most important but also the most difficult parameter to measure. In measuring impact, find out what the overall impact of the campaign has been on the organization. The impact of a campaign can be the results of an election, a change in the perception of the organization and its reputation, or the financial performance of the company. Returning to the example of a political campaign, if you count election results among the outcomes, in the case of impact evaluation you are interested in the number of seats won in a parliament, the change in the party's reputation or the concrete contribution to funding.

The Barcelona Principles also lean towards measuring results using the method above. These are a set of seven principles introduced by the International Association for the Measurement and Evaluation of Communication (AMEC) in 2010 that recommend how to effectively measure the value of communication. Given the high dynamics of public relations, AMEC has already revised the principles twice. The latest version, the Barcelona Principles 3.0, was introduced by the association in 2020. This is their text:

BARCELONA PRINCIPLES 3.0

1. *Setting goals is an absolute prerequisite to communications planning, measurement and evaluation*

The founding principle of SMART (specific, measurable, actionable, relevant, and time-bound) goals as a foundation for communications planning has been promoted to an essential prerequisite. It pushes measurement and evaluation as a core component of the planning process, articulating target outcomes and how progress towards these will be assessed.

2. *Measurement and evaluation should identify outputs, outcomes and potential impact*

Previously, the Principles recommended measuring outcomes, rather than simply counting outputs. The updated principles extend this to consider longer term impact of communications strategy. According to Levine, this means thinking about 'the channels we are impacting, and change we would like to see through campaigns, events and activations'.

How to Set SMART Goals?

SMART goals are a very practical method for designing specific objectives in the management and planning of (not only) PR campaigns. Let's imagine how these goals work, using the example of a model PR campaign for personal branding of a certain CEO. The SMART objectives of such a campaign would be:

Specific: What do you want to accomplish? What is to happen and for what reasons are you creating the campaign?

Measurable: What indicators will you choose? For example, you can target the number of outputs, reach, type of media, number of social media posts, or participation in conferences. However, it is always necessary to identify measurable indicators for the campaign.

Achievable: Is it within your financial, media or personal capacity and ability to achieve the goal?

Relevant: Are the objectives of the campaign interesting to the target group and the client? Do they make sense?

Time-bound: You need to identify the timeframe in which you want to prepare, deliver, measure, and evaluate the campaign.

3. Outcomes and impact should be identified for stakeholders, society, and the organization

From the original focus on business metrics, such as sales and revenue, the 2020 update embraces a more holistic view of performance. It allows the model to be more inclusive of a broader range of organizations and communications roles that are not necessarily profit-driven.

4. Communication measurement and evaluation should include both qualitative and quantitative analysis

'To understand the full impact of your work, it is crucial that you use the full suite of methods to measure those outcomes', summarized Levine in describing the evolution of this principle to not just quantify but also understand how messages are being received, believed and interpreted.

5. AVEs are not the value of communication

The message remains consistent and clear; 'we continue to believe that AVEs do not demonstrate the value of our work'. It is important that communications measurement and evaluation employs a richer, more nuanced, and multi-faceted approach to understand the impact of communications.

6. Holistic communication measurement and evaluation includes all relevant online and offline channels

Our founding principle that social media can and should be measured is so obvious today. The 2020 iteration reflects the game-changing shift in social communications' capabilities, opportunities, and influence, such that all relevant online and offline channels should be measured and evaluated equally. The AMEC measurement framework promotes clarity across earned, owned, shared, and paid channels to ensure consistency in approach towards a common goal.

7. Communication measurement and evaluation are rooted in integrity and transparency to drive learning and insights

Sound, consistent and sustained measurement calls for integrity and transparency in recognition of today's attention to data privacy and stewardship as organizations comply with new regulations, such as GDPR. This is also a statement that measurement isn't simply about data collection and tracking, but about learning from evaluation and applying insight back into communications planning. It recognizes the need to be transparent about the context in which programmes are run and being aware of any bias that may exist in the tools, methodologies and interpretations applied.

Organizations that want to become market leaders should take the Barcelona Principles into account in all their communication campaign planning. This can be a challenge – contemporary communication is specific in that, compared to the past, it includes an increasing number of communication tools and activities that companies should measure. Another challenge is how to measure these tools and activities, as each has its own metrics. Thus, the result of measuring communication will not be a single number – nor should it be.

What does this imply? You probably can't effectively set the right goals and metrics during an afternoon coffee break. But if we go back to Richard Bagnall's initial prediction, you'll at least be assured that the job won't make you even busier fools. Smart goal setting, in short, is one of those activities that will pay you back many times over. As entrepreneur, philanthropist and billionaire Bob Parsons said, 'If it was easy, everyone would be doing it, and you wouldn't have an opportunity'.

LEAD GENERATION

In the chapter on PR measurement, of course, we can't forget the popular metric that divides communication content into two categories according to the goal it leads to. Those categories are *thought leadership and lead generation.*

LEAD GENERATION

SOURCE: LeadershipLabNow.com

Let's imagine a campaign to launch a new type of camera, with all the manufacturer's materials – photos, infographics, datasheets and technical specifications – at our disposal. In such a case, PR professionals usually rush to promote the brand's thought leadership. That is, they will do everything they can to ensure that the brand has a reputation with the public as an authority in the field, an expert, even a trendsetter. They will therefore prepare a press release, organize a camera launch in the form of an attractive 'hands-on' press conference, create articles for the media, offer products for journalists to review, launch collaborations with influencers and, of course, social media communication. In short, speaking through the lens of the PESO Model™, most capable PR professionals have PES, i.e. paid, earned and shared media, in mind.

When ignoring the O part, i.e. owned media, however, PR professionals are walking past the opportunity to make achieving the goal much easier. It is the channel they can control and thus ensure there is a consistent and controllable message reaching stakeholders.

PR campaign without owned media is literally like the dog without a tail. We shouldn't forget that in public relations, it is the tail that can wag the whole dog. Actually, this is what profaned phrase 'wag the dog' used to mean: something insignificant taking over the role of something very significant.

Owned media helps us to generate leads, i.e. relevant contacts/people who have the potential to turn into customers. There are countless ways to generate leads – people can subscribe to a newsletter, download an ebook, sign up for a webinar. . . It is true that leads can be collected also through other channels of the PESO Model™, but none of them give us as much control as owned media. Moreover, leads can be the fuel that drives genuine market leadership. So don't underestimate the value of investing in owned media.

PRICING ACCORDING TO THE VALUE OF PR

Indeed, measuring the value that PR brings to companies will in the future become not only a way to measure and evaluate public relations, but also to price it. Currently, the services that PR agencies deliver to their clients are largely charged on a time basis.

The principle is simple. The agency simply estimates the time taken by a given activity, assigns an adequate hourly rate (depending on whether the activity is handled by a junior or requires the know-how of a senior employee), and calculates the price of the service based on these parameters. Clients are then charged for the hours worked, or are charged a monthly flat rate that includes a pre-agreed amount of work (of course, there can be many more models of collaboration, but these are the most common ones).

Setting an hourly rate is therefore the alpha and omega of how PR agencies operate. And it's an easy model for clients to understand. However, charging on an 'hourly' basis does come with pitfalls. How long something takes to do is not a measure of the value delivered. So, time based charging makes it very hard for clients and agencies to demonstrate a return on investment from the money spent on communications.

Pricing according to the value to be delivered may be the solution. That is, identify how the outcome and impact can be evaluated and price to achieve this. Indeed, a well-chosen goal can be easily quantified in monetary terms: what is the value of a job applicant, a new subscriber to a service or even 'just' an email from a potential customer... In this case, the agency can choose a remuneration model that depends on the value that its work brings, e.g. the number and quality of leads. Tim Williams of Ignition Consulting Group describes this principle perfectly when he says: 'Clients don't buy your activities or costs. They buy results, value and benefit'. Yet the relationship between cost and value is often a tangled one. It's illustrated by a story that many PR managers have probably experienced.

COST VS. VALUE

A client of our agency was facing a potential crisis. One article published in a well-known media outlet treated potential damage to the client's reputation. There was only one solution. I picked up the phone, spoke to the journalist, the journalist rewrote the article based on the facts presented, and the crisis was averted. How simple! The situation was resolved by a single phone call, the cost of which was maybe tens of dollars – let's say a quarter of an hour of my time. But the difference the call made was significant, probably saving the client millions. How to approach such a huge disparity between cost and value? The solution to the dilemma is to set reward rules up front, perhaps by setting a percentage reward on the value the agency brings or saves.

Some campaigns are ideal for this approach. A great example is the campaign my agency and I created for Wood & Company. This leading Czech investment management company wanted to expand its client base. Since research showed that Czechs often lack knowledge about investing in general, we decided to create a simple way to increase public interest in investing while bringing new clients to Wood & Company's investment platform Portu – an online test! It was a great way to help people understand the basics of investing and test their knowledge at the same time. Using an online survey, we created a benchmark we called the Investment Literacy Index. To bring credibility, we secured support for the index calculation method from four influential investment analysts. We then created a microsite with a test that people could complete themselves and compare their scores to the national average. The campaign was accompanied by activities in other types of media channels, particularly earned and paid media, which generated interest and traffic to the microsite. In just three months, we achieved three times the original campaign goal, with around 300 people creating an account on the investment platform Portu and the campaign generating €250,000 in revenue – 26 times the agency's time-based fee. If we had taken a few percent of the profit then, it would still have been a multiple of what we actually earned. This is a typical example of what a well-set up value-based campaign can deliver, and a real story of why so many agencies prefer to play it safe. In short, we didn't trust ourselves.

The value of the PR professionals is not only in the time and effort they put into their work. It lies mainly in the expertise, the know-how accumulated over the years and the value that our work brings. However, selling a PR service not on the basis of effort delivered but value delivered takes business acumen and, above all, courage – something I lacked when creating proposition for Wood

& Company. You can never be 100% sure that the work would pay off. The uncertainty is not the only obstacle.

Creating a value-based proposition is quite complex and, above all, demanding. Agencies need to know their clients and their potential very well, or, by asking good questions, find out what goals a particular organization has and what value they see in the results of a campaign. The ball is not only in the agencies' court: a willingness on the client's part to share the necessary data, information about the company's operations and business model is also essential. As the return on investment of a campaign can take time, they also need to enter into a longer-term contract with the agency. Such decisions no longer rest solely on the shoulders of the marketing and communications departments, but the key goals for the organization set by the C-level managers or the Board. Instead of the number of clicks, PR campaigns aim for the number of leads, products sold and the real impact on the organization's operations. *A well thought out brief, and mutual trust across the organization, is essential to the future value that PR will bring.*

In the future, we are likely to see both models of pricing the work of a PR professional. We cannot expect time-based charging to disappear completely. In some aspects of PR work, it will continue to be the most practical solution – for example, in executive services, crisis communications, etc. The same applies to the value-based pricing model. It simply cannot be automatically applied to all scenarios. However, when applied to the right type of campaign, a remuneration model based on value delivered, a clearly defined impact of the campaign on the organization, incentivizes clients and PR agencies to run more effective campaigns, which deliver higher rewards to both parties... and ultimately ensures that every cent spent actually turns into leadership dollars.

THE ESSENTIAL STEPS TO ENSURE EVERY CENT YOU SPEND TURNS INTO A LEADERSHIP DOLLAR

1. *When measuring PR, follow the Barcelona Principles.* If you want to become a market leader, you should take these rules into account when planning all your communication campaigns.

2. *Stop counting AVE.* Converting editorial space to equivalent advertising value does not show the value of PR work.

3. *Use the AMEC evaluation framework to measure the impact of campaigns.* It's a very useful tool to help you make consistent progress towards your communications goal.

4. *Be systematic and categorize the results achieved.* The categories of outputs, out-takes, outcomes and impact will help you to assess the results of your campaign. Take these aspects into account when planning the communication itself.

5. *Consider a reward model based on value delivered.* Hourly rates and charging for activities delivered will soon be a thing of the past. Stay one step ahead and deliver real value, not effort. Everyone will benefit.

6

HOW TO SATISFY STAKEHOLDERS' DESIRE TO SAVE THE WORLD?

Sustainability, Brand Activism and the Purpose of Organizations

How your organization approaches *social issues, the environment and everything happening in the world is more important than ever.* It determines how your company is perceived by employees, candidates, investors, partners and customers. Don't be fooled into thinking that you can satisfy stakeholders' desire to save the world by simply opting for either CSR, sustainability reporting, diversity or awareness campaigns. You can't pick just one and neglect the others. Everything must be connected and spring from a common foundation, which is the purpose of the organization. This is what influences the behaviour of the company in every aspect of its operations and ultimately all its stakeholders. In the future all key stakeholders will decide whether to devote their time, energy, and money to your organization, or not, based on the purpose and its real impact.

* * * * *

SUSTAINABILITY BECOMES AN INTEGRAL PART OF OUR MINDSET

Scott Chaikin

Picture a hockey stick graph. In the evolution of corporate sustainability, we are currently at the point where the line first turns upward. The question of what the graph looks like over the next 20 years is how steeply it will climb – how quickly sustainability will become completely integrated into everyday business thinking and operation.

20 years ago, sustainability – defined as 'development that meets the needs of the present without compromising the ability of future generations to meet their own needs' – was struggling to find its place on the world stage. The UN Global Compact, which provided a practical framework for companies committed to sustainability and responsible business practices, was only launched in 2000. In 2006, 100 of the world's largest institutional investors signed on to adopt the UN Principles for Responsible Investing (PRI). Around the same time the term Environmental, Social, Governance (ESG) was coined, based on the assumption that ESG factors (environmental, social, governance) have financial relevance. In 2015, the UN established 17 Sustainable Development Goals for 2030, including not just areas like climate action, clean water, and affordable clean energy but also zero poverty or hunger, good health and well-being, gender equality, reduced inequality, peace, justice and strong institutions.

Meanwhile, huge stakeholder groups like employees, customers and investors became impatient, driven in part by the ever more visible impacts of worsening climate conditions. While employees and customers report that sustainability has increasing influence over their decisions about companies they'll work for or buy from, it's easier to quantify investor behaviour. According to Bloomberg, ESG investment – which grew from $23 to $38 trillion between 2016 and 2021 – will hit $53 trillion by 2025, or one-third of all assets under management. The UN's PRI has gone from having 100 institutional investors as signatories to 4,000. In 2011 20% of companies in the US S&P 500 reported on sustainability; today over 90% do so.

While the typical company today is wrestling with what (and how) to measure and report on ESG, adoption and sophistication are accelerating as stakeholder interest demands it. That acceleration will only quicken in the years ahead. Government regulations and ESG and sustainability mandates are growing around the world. In the US, the Securities and Exchange Commission has proposed that all US public companies disclose their greenhouse gas emissions and climate-change mitigation actions. It will be less than 20 years before environmental reporting becomes as routine and closely audited as financial data.

At the same time, influence and power will increasingly flow to members of Gen Z and Gen Y, for whom sustainability, diversity and inclusion, and corporate social responsibility have always been more important.

Alongside stakeholder influence, technology will enable climate and other solutions that are only imaginable today. And financial results will continue to show what they already do: companies with strong ESG ratings outperform those with lower ratings.

What will we say about sustainability 20 years from now? The easy part is knowing that sustainability will have become a fundamental part of every business, service, initiative and product. While governments demand increasingly sustainable practices, customer and employee support will diminish for companies that fail to adopt them. And, as investors have already come to understand that a company that isn't run responsibly for all its shareholders isn't being run well enough for its investors, the increasing influence of ESG on investment capital will ensure that responsibility, not just profitability, helps determine who deserves to be winners and losers.

One of the primary attributes of companies that succeed over the next 20 years will be strong ESG performance, because it is what investors, customers, employees and governments will demand.

✳ ✳ ✳ ✳ ✳

> *While governments demand increasingly sustainable practices, customer and employee support will diminish for companies that fail to adopt them.*

Who Is Scott Chaikin

Scott Chaikin's career is primarily associated with Dix & Eaton, where he has worked for nearly 37 years, currently as Executive Chairman. He specializes in counsel to senior leadership on communications surrounding critical issues and major change initiatives. His work has focused on CEO succession, crises, culture change, M&A, rebranding and shareholder activism. He has created communications strategies for companies such as Akzo-Nobel, American Greetings, Covia, Federal Reserve Bank of Cleveland, Forest City Realty Trust, Keycorp, Northwest Airlines, Rock and Roll Hall of Fame, and UnitedHealth Group.

MAKING YOUR COMMITMENT TO ESG AN INGREDIENT FOR LEADERSHIP SUCCESS

The trends really do speak volumes. Whereas organizations used to focus purely on CSR, today their 'doing good' needs to be much more comprehensive. ESG, *the continuous strategic effort to measure, evaluate and benchmark the impact of our business on society and the planet, is coming to the fore*. If you want to become a market leader and outperform your competitors, you should definitely not only know this new mantra of sustainability, but more importantly, reflect it in your company's operations.

ESG is an acronym for environment, social and governance and describes the process by which a company evaluates its performance on environmental, social and governance issues. By taking a comprehensive approach to business impact, ESG correctly demonstrates that sustainability is not just about buying recycled paper for the printer but touches on everything from the environment (carbon footprint, emissions, water savings), social issues (diversity, equity, inclusion) to corporate governance itself (financial transparency, openness, but also efficient use of resources).

Whether your company is involved in industrial production, sells software or provides consultancy, sustainability will affect it in the years to come. ESG expects us all to become proactive about the impact our business has on people and the world around us. And so, we'll be forced to think about whether manufacturing waste can be reprocessed, whether all the business travel is really necessary, or how we can better insulate our office. We'll all be calculating our carbon footprint – if not for our own purposes, it's very likely that one of our partners or customers will soon be asking about it.

In fact, CO_2 measurement usually distinguishes three categories, called scopes. The first category measures direct emissions from owned or controlled sources (e.g. emissions from company cars, boilers or emissions from the disposal of waste produced by the company). The second category includes CO_2 emissions from purchased energy that are not generated directly by the company but are a direct result of company activities (this includes, in particular, the purchase of electricity, heat or steam). Companies that are serious about sustainability then include in their carbon footprint all emissions generated in the company's complete value chain – scope 3.

Clearly, this third category of emissions measurement affects us all. So you should expect, and plan for, your customers asking you about your holistic carbon footprint. As Scott Chaikin writes, companies that can integrate ESG principles into their operations will be valued by consumers, investors, governments and our planet. I can add to his already telling data: According to EY's global survey from late 2020, investor interest in non-financial information has increased by a staggering 30% over the past two years. For 91% of them, ESG parameters even play a key role in deciding whether to invest in a given project or company. The global value shift is apparent across all stakeholder groups. This means one thing: *Companies that do not address and communicate their sustainability activities will soon cease to be of interest to all the stakeholders that control their future success.*

Companies that do not address and communicate their sustainability activities will soon cease to be of interest to all the stakeholders that control their future success.

HOW TO DECIDE WHAT 'GOOD' YOU WILL DO

So how do you approach the desire of your customers, investors and other stakeholders to save our hard-pressed planet? The mission of companies to 'do good' and the areas of communications and marketing that this involves are nicely summarized in the matrix below. It neatly divides 'doing good' according to how inward or outward facing it is, and also illustrates the interconnectedness of all areas. As you can see from the matrix, in addition to CSR (and, more importantly, ESG, which also belongs in the same box), it is critically important for organizations to define their purpose (we will therefore discuss how and why to find the company mission shortly). It is only on the basis of their purpose that companies can take positions on the issues and problems of the world around us. So-called brand activism, i.e. the involvement of organizations in social, political or environmental issues, is an area of growing importance and as such will also be given a place at the end of this chapter. However, the described matrix is of course only one of the possible approaches.

Business as a Force for Good

Getting our House in Order

E.g. ethical supply chains, sustainability, workers' rights, consumer value

Adapted from: Sarkar, C. and Kotler, P. (2018) 'Brand Activism: From Purpose to Action' Idea Bite Press: USA.

In this sense, ESG partially replaces traditional CSR in its long-term and strategic dimension. For brands that are serious about sustainability, it is also the first step on the road to becoming a better (or good) 'citizen'. The first step is simply to get your own house in order. A good starting communication tool is sustainability reporting (sometimes also called non-financial reporting). Unlike typical reports full of economic results, sustainability reporting focuses on the less economic, yet quantifiable areas of a company's operations. For example, its impact on the environment, its social impact, or its staff diversity. There are several reasons for embarking on sustainability reporting.

WHAT DOES SUSTAINABILITY REPORTING BRING YOU?

1. *You get useful data*

Investing in the data collection needed for sustainability reporting not only serves the external presentation, but also the company itself. It will pay off in other areas as well. You can use sustainability reporting to improve management and planning, create strategic goals, identify risks and integrate desired values into your company culture. The report can thus do your company a great service.

2. *You attract investors*

In EY's late 2020 global survey, 75% of investors said that corporate sustainability is a sign that their investments are safe and have the potential for long-term growth. If you want to inspire investor confidence, you can't do without ESG.

3. *You will please stakeholders*

The global value shift is not only visible to investors. Where a company stands on non-financial issues, especially sustainability, becomes an important value for all stakeholders, be they employees, partners, customers and other stakeholders. Accommodating them means accommodating future winning tenders and swaying many other decisions in your favour – such as who they buy from, where they choose to work or who they choose as a supplier.

4. *You will be a leader in sustainability*

Brands that are serious about sustainability have a better public image. According to EY's 2021 #FutureConsumerIndex research, brand social responsibility is important to 52% of consumers. Up to 68% of consumers think companies should make a positive impact on the world, and 50% of consumers in 20 countries add that they would prefer to buy from companies that disclose the impact their products have on people and the planet. Starting sustainability reporting early is a way to get an important head start in this area.

5. *You get communication material*

The data you get from non-financial reporting can be used effectively in other communications. Sustainability generates interest, which you will capitalize on in marketing, PR or social media communications.

Given that sustainability is likely to be a very important topic for your stakeholders (and the future will intensify this), the role of PR is almost indispensable in this respect. Communications professionals can play a key role in embedding ESG in an organization and setting an ESG strategy. It is effective communication that will complete your efforts to convince stakeholders that your company is well prepared for the sustainability challenges of the future.

It should be added, however, that the topic of sustainability, or non-financial reporting, is not just an exercise for the communications and CSR department. The foundation must be based on the company's core strategy and the decisions of top management. It is the management of the organization that has to take everything I have mentioned in the previous paragraphs at face value, start behaving according to the rules of sustainability and guide the company by them. It is the only way. Otherwise, if management 'does good' only in its polished reports, the sustainability effort will collapse like a house of cards across the entire organization. Then stakeholder trust risks disappearing in the rubble along with it. How are they supposed to trust that the organization is authentic on other issues?

* * * * *

HOW WILL BEING PURPOSE-DRIVEN SEPARATE LEADERS FROM THE REST?

Crispin Manners

Sue Garrard, when at Unilever, said: 'The world of big business is dividing into those who really have a clear sense of how their business adds value to society and those who see their sole objective to be purely economic by delivering short term value to shareholders'.

Simon Sinek famously said on a TED Talk: 'People don't buy what you do; they buy why you do it. And what you do simply proves what you believe'.

And that may be why James Mitchell, Former Managing Director at Innocent Drinks, said this about Purpose: 'Purpose is a currency far more valuable than stock options or cash. When an individual finds the "why" it's powerful. When a team finds it, they become an unstoppable force'.

These quotes are clear indicators of why being purpose-driven will deliver a significant leadership advantage. But why is Purpose so important? And what happens if your behaviour proves the leaders of the business doesn't believe in it?

In the age of ultra-transparency having a phoney purpose will be a source of failure.

People recognise that not every organisation's purpose is to cure cancer, but they expect that the organisation will make choices that have a positive impact on people, the community and the planet. And in the age of ultra-transparency – where every action is scrutinised - the difference a company makes needs to be transparent and explicit – and it must come from the authentic values that are embedded deep in the DNA of the organisation.

So, let's look at when actions seem to conflict with words. P&O Ferries has this as their mission: 'Our mission is to build the best possible business for our customers, our people and our communities'. In March 2022, the company's CEO sacked 800 staff via video call and replaced them with contract workers on about half the UK's minimum wage. These actions, as Sinek would say, simply proves what P&O Ferries believes – and it doesn't appear to support its mission. The negative commercial and reputational impact of these actions will be long-lasting.

Purpose is the foundation for sustainable leadership.

The Worldcom Confidence Index charts what over 100,000 CEOs are thinking each month. Three topics are consistently in the top five – retaining talent, sustainability and the economy. An authentic purpose, that comes from the hearts of the leadership, can address all three of these challenges. Here are a few reasons why.

- *Humans have a fundamental need for purpose*

The need for purpose is one of the defining characteristics of human beings. We crave purpose and can suffer serious psychological difficulties without it. Research commissioned by the John Templeton Foundation found that purpose 'is a central component of most leading conceptions of optimal human development and psychological well-being'.[1]

This extract from their post above is a good example of how a sense of purpose can make a difference at both a personal and organisational level.

'A sense of purpose in one's career is correlated with both greater satisfaction at work as well as better work-related outputs. In a 2001 study of service workers, researchers indicated that some hospital cleaning staff considered themselves 'mere janitors' while others thought of themselves as part of the overall team that brought healing to patients. These groups of individuals performed the same basic tasks, but they thought very differently about their

---

[1]Adolescent Moral Development Lab at Claremont Graduate University (2018) *The psychology of purpose*. Prosocial Consulting and the John Templeton Foundation.

sense of purpose in the organizations where they worked. Not surprisingly, the workers who viewed their role as having a healing function were more satisfied with their jobs, spent more time with patients, worked more closely with doctors and nurses, and found more meaning in their jobs.

- ### Shared purpose at work can be transformational

This means that purpose is powerful for companies. A study published by the Harvard Business Review showed that companies that had a clear purpose had better growth compared with companies that didn't. But perhaps most telling for the world we live in today, purpose-driven companies experienced more than three times the level of success in major transformation efforts (52% compared with 16%). And this research is from before the pandemic. Since then, the need to change or transform the way we all operate has become paramount.

- ### World events are making us all think about our purpose in life

The pandemic, the latest UN report on the 'irreversible impacts of climate change', and the war in Ukraine, are making each of us think about the difference we want to make and how we can be a force for good. As one Forbes article put it: 'Nothing raises questions concerning life's purpose like facing mortality'.

So, every day, your people will bring both these conscious and unconscious thoughts to work. Like the hospital cleaners above, they will be looking to connect what they do every day to a purpose they believe in, and they will want to feel they work with people who believe the same things.

If leaders want to succeed, they will need to explain what they believe (their purpose) so they attract people who believe it to. And they will have to show how the success of the organisation contributes to all key stakeholders – people, society, the planet and shareholders.

* * * * *

In the age of ultra-transparency having a phoney purpose will be a source of failure.

Who Is Crispin Manners

The purpose should be an indispensable part of the company's goals and plans. This is the motto of Crispin Manners, a PR professional with more than 40 years of experience in the field. In 2010, he became a founding fellow of the PRCA, having previously been its chairman. He led his PR firm to become  the fastest growing PR company in the UK and created an award-winning communications planning and management regime (ValueFlow) that won for his firm the accolade of the UK's Innovative Company of the Year in 2003. He is a Director of the Worldcom PR Group and Chairman of Inspiring Workplaces Group – an organization with the purpose of changing the world by transforming the world of work.

WHERE TO FIND A PURPOSE

First of all, one thing must be stated. Not all leaders recognize the need to express a *purpose*, a factor so fundamental to the leadership that Crispin Manners talks about. There are certainly many successful companies with content employees and satisfactory performance, and yet these companies do not have a defined or publicly stated purpose. On the other hand, there are also plenty of organizations that have their purpose carved deeply into their foundation (as well as their values, goals, and business plan) and whose owners have been astute, enlightened, or passionate enough about why the organization exists and the value it delivers to its stakeholders to reflect that purpose in all aspects of the company from the very beginning.

Either way, proclaimed or not, organization's purpose is the reason why it exists. It is an expression of the value it expects to deliver to all its stakeholders. This could be make as much money for shareholders as possible – nothing bad about it. But in today's world, for all the reasons Crispin Manners expressed in his forecast, most stakeholders, both internal and external, want to see the company they support be a force for good in some way or another. They want to believe in what they do, invest in or stay behind. Here are three examples of such belief from agency employees Crispin Manner works with

'I believe we are helping to improve the health of the nation'.
'I believe we are helping to make Ireland a fairer society'.
'I believe we helping disruptive technology companies cross the chasm so they can make a real difference in the world'.

If we want to excel as leaders, we can't do without a purpose. It helps a company navigate a changing and unpredictable environment and deliver higher and more sustainable performance. Indeed, the purpose, if explicitly explained, is the guide that helps an organization find its voice in the public debate.

In case you don't have a purpose coded right into the DNA of the company, you will have to surface what the leadership believes in and identify the value the organization delivers to all stakeholders. This used to be straightforward because leaders saw their stakeholders as a tightly defined group. And they saw the good they did as an implicit part of what they did. But the future world has much more complex expectations. The world of work now embraces the world outside work. And as the chapter on ESG explained, even investors who exist to make money, care about how that money is made.

Hubert Joly, former chairman and CEO of Best Buy and a lecturer at Harvard Business School, sums up how to do it nicely in his article *Creating a Meaningful Corporate Purpose* (Harvard Business Review). According to him, the following five aspects need to be considered to define a strong corporate purpose.

1. *Look for your Company Purpose at the Intersection of the Four Circles*

While much is said and written about a company's purpose, it is not always well understood what it actually is. Hubert Joly offers this definition of corporate purpose: it is the ultimate goal of a company, the fundamental reason it exists and how it contributes to the common good.

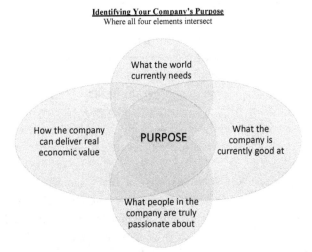

Identifying Your Company's Purpose
Where all four elements intersect

What the world currently needs

How the company can deliver real economic value

PURPOSE

What the company is currently good at

What people in the company are truly passionate about

Adapted from: Joly, H. & Lambert, C. (2021) The Heart of Business: Leadership Principles for the Next Era of Capitalism. Harvard Business Review Press: Brighton, Massachusetts, USA.

To create a meaningful, authentic, credible and powerful purpose statement, thoroughly examine all four circles of the picture. It is at their intersection that you will find your direction. In this process, it is good to consider:

What the world needs: What specific, important and unmet needs exist in the world? How critical is it to address these needs? What change will this bring about?

What are the people in the company passionate about: What drives the people in the company? What change do they want to make in the world? (These questions apply to senior leadership as well as to all employees.)

What makes the company unique: What are the unique strengths that allow your company to address certain needs in a way that others cannot? How does your organization need to evolve/expand to address selected needs in this unique way?

How can the company create economic value: what business opportunities arise from these considerations? How attractive are the associated potential profit pools? Can the company capture enough of this value?

2. Anchor the Company's Purpose in Underlying Human Needs

In defining the company's purpose, it is critical to focus on human needs, not the products and services you offer to meet them. First, it's much more inspiring. In the words of Simon Sinek and his aforementioned TED talk, this is what separates the WHY from the WHAT and the HOW. Second, this approach broadens a company's horizons and opens up other areas of the market.

3. Connect the Purpose to What Matters to You and Your Team

Don't be afraid to put personal goals into your purpose. Business is inherently about people. If you see your business as a human organization made up of individuals working together towards a common goal, one thing is essential: leaders at all levels must be clear about why they work, and they must also understand what drives the people around them.

The personal approach has another important advantage: it illuminates what people in the company, from the front-liners to the top management, enjoy. When people's passions align with the company's purpose, then everyone gives their best to pursue that collective purpose.

4. Embrace All Stakeholders in a Declaration of Interdependence

The question of what the world needs touches employees, customers, suppliers, communities and company stakeholders. According to Hubert Joly, a business cannot thrive in the long term if the planet or community is on fire or if employees are unhappy. Business cannot succeed in isolation.

How can companies ensure that all stakeholders benefit from the company's purpose? First, they need to clearly identify who their stakeholders are, what they need, and how the company could help meet those needs. Such a view of business goes beyond the four walls of the company and mobilizes all stakeholders to achieve the company's purpose. Business is then viewed as an ecosystem based on the mutually beneficial interdependence of all stakeholders. At the heart of this system are the employees. It is they who create and develop authentic relationships both within the company and with all stakeholders.

To do this, we need to reject business as a zero-sum game. Brian Chesky, co-founder and CEO of Airbnb, puts it nicely, 'This idea that for one stakeholder to win, another has to lose is, to me, bad design. I always think like a designer. Design is not the way something looks; design is how something works, and something works best when it works for the largest number of people'.

5. Choose the Right Level of Ambition

A company's purpose should be neither too ambitious nor too modest, but just ambitious enough. A goal that is too disconnected from the company's core business or is so broad or vague that it could apply to any other company is likely to remain an empty statement. At the other end of the spectrum, a purpose that describes what the company is already doing, rather than addressing an unsolved problem, is unlikely to change much or inspire anyone.

How do you know if you've decided on the right company purpose? Once you come up with a possible formulation, you need to make sure that the result of all the thinking and searching is not just an empty phrase. To avoid this, ask if your purpose is:

- *Meaningful.* Does it have real meaning for people's lives? Does it have the potential to make a meaningful difference for all stakeholders?

- *Authentic.* Does it match what people in the company care deeply about? Does it align with the company's values and behaviours?

- *Credible.* Does it leverage the company's unique capabilities or assets? Can the company achieve results that significantly change the status quo? Does it make business sense?

- *Powerful.* Are the needs the company addresses important? How much good comes from addressing these needs?

- *Compelling.* Is it clear, specific and ambitious enough to inspire and mobilize people inside and outside the company?

But formulation is only the first step. Next, you need to start translating your purpose into real action, and not just in Power-Point presentations and on the company website. The company's purpose should become the cornerstone of its strategy and should be embraced by all employees. Last but not least, we need to create an environment where everyone is able and willing to give their best to support the purpose. This is the only way to build a truly meaningful company, concludes Hubert Joly.

I couldn't agree more. I would also add that a clearly defined purpose is very important for effective purpose-driven communication campaigning, along with alignment with values and authenticity. Going forward, the purpose statement and its implementation to real actions will become increasingly important as it helps an organization to position itself towards its stakeholders. If you want to keep your company at the top, the work of fulfilling your corporate purpose never ends. Who else should lead this process than PR managers?

COMPONENTS OF A PURPOSE-DRIVEN CAMPAIGN

Which of the following do you believe are the most important components of an effective purpose-driven campaign?

#	Component	%
1	Authentic messaging	47 %
2	Fit with values of the brand	45 %
3	Clear statement of purpose	40 %
4	Long-term commitment	35 %
5	Relevance to customers	26 %
6	Internal employee engagement	25 %
7	Call to action	24 %
8	Continuity with our legacy	15 %
9	Partnership with activist groups	13 %
10	Differentiation in marketplace	11 %

SOURCE: 2022 Global Communication Report, USC Annenberg Center for Public Relations

* * * * *

POLARIZATION HAS CREATED A NEW REALITY FOR THE PR PROFESSION

Fred Cook

Every year, at the University of Southern California (USC) we conduct a global survey to forecast the future of public relations. We research the trends that are shaping the profession and impacting those who work in it. In the past, we've examined advancements in technology, the changing media landscape and the evolution of ethics.

Our reports always paint a picture of a dynamic industry. But now the stakes are even higher. Continued political conflict—on top of an extended global pandemic—has created a new reality for the PR profession. Media has become more biased, information has become more unreliable, and opinions have become more extreme. As a result, our society seems to be permanently polarized.

In today's world, polarization is a more complex, multi-dimensional phenomenon and the forces that spread it have created a divide that is more toxic and more permanent. Polarization is no longer just the result of disagreements. It's the cause of them.

In the past few years, societal discord has become a significant risk factor for global business, posing a threat to corporate reputation, employee recruitment, and organizational morale. In response, CEOs, who have embraced stakeholder capitalism, are now recognizing they have the responsibility— and the platform—to engage with controversial topics outside of their normal comfort zones.

Professional communicators are the pioneers in this unfamiliar territory. About 93% are spending more time navigating a growing list of complex societal topics. The majority are looking to their employees to determine their positions. All of them are making difficult daily decisions that have serious, long-term impact on their companies and their communities. Public relations has never been more demanding or more meaningful.

* * * * *

> *Polarization is no longer just the result of disagreements. It's the cause of them.*

Who Is Fred Cook

A cabin boy on a Norwegian tanker, a doorman at a five-star hotel or chauffeur for drunks. For a long time, Fred Cook's career did not suggest that he would one day be a recognized communications expert and PR Week would include him in the list of the 50 most powerful people in PR. But his life experiences have  helped him become a true public relations professional. For more than 35 years, he has worked at the Golin Agency, where he has managed clients for world-famous brands (Nintendo, Toyota and Disney) and worked with major business leaders such as Herb Kelleher, Jeff Bezos and Steve Jobs. Since 2015, he has been the Director of the USC Center for Public Relations at the Annenberg School. Fred Cook is also the author of *Improvise: Unconventional Career Advice from an Unlikely CEO*.

FUTURE LEADERS WILL ENGAGE WITH SOCIAL ISSUES

We have already discussed a range of communications challenges to be overcome by tomorrow's leaders. This chapter addresses one of the most significant, the engagement with social issues. An increasing proportion of the public expects brands to actively contribute to the common good. This is borne out by data from the USC study Fred Cook discusses, which was conducted with a sample of 1,600 professional communicators, journalists, students and educators. Exactly 82% of respondents believe that businesses are responsible for the well-being of their employees and customers and that maintaining social harmony is their responsibility.

This is closely linked to the development of a concept called stakeholder capitalism: a vision of capitalism in which organizations do not only serve their shareholders but are tasked with satisfying a wide range of stakeholders – customers, employees, partners and even local communities, in addition to shareholders. Such a mission obviously requires a change in approach to business. Companies should emphasize the creation of long-term value that will have a positive effect on as many stakeholders as possible – profit with a purpose if you will. It is these values – which undoubtedly include social responsibility and commitment – that will replace the pursuit of short-term profits that have so far served only a narrow group of stakeholders. In the wake of recent social upheavals, more and more leaders are calling for a turn towards stakeholder capitalism. These include, for example, Klaus Schwab, president and founder of the World Economic Forum.

The turn in values away from pure profit to profit with a purpose and social responsibility is, of course, also reflected in the work of communications professionals. A USC study shows that 73% of PR professionals expect to increase their engagement on social issues in the coming year. Three times more are working with activist groups than three years ago. Looking again at the matrix *Business as a force for good* in the beginning of this chapter, this indicates an increase in activities that have a high impact on the organization both inward and outward.

THE POTENTIAL OF PURPOSE

To what extent do you agree or disagree with the following statements?

83 %	Business has a powerful platform it can use to speak from on important issues.
82 %	Business has a vested interest in maintaining a cohesive/harmonious society.
82 %	Business is responsible for the health, well-being and welfare of millions of employees.
78 %	Business has a responsibility to support causes and speak out on issues that align with their brand purpose/mission.
75 %	Business has resources to solve some of the country's biggest problems.
67 %	Business has a rational voice that can communicate with the public on sensitive topics more easily than the government.
67 %	Business reflects the values of millions of employees and customers.

Strongly or somewhat AGREE

SOURCE: 2022 Global Communication Report.
USC Annenberg Center for Public Relations

SOCIAL POLARIZATION AS A CHALLENGE FOR PUBLIC RELATIONS

But it will not be without risk. In fact, ideas about what the desired 'social good' is (and what brand activism should look like) have never been so different. The unprecedented *polarization of society* that we currently face makes brand activism a potentially polarising enterprise. As Fred Cook writes: Polarization is no longer just the result of disagreement. It is the cause. That's why 77% of professionals see it as a challenge for their organization.

The main, and understandable, concern that polarization brings, is alienating people. One good example is the issue of abortion, which is stirring the American public. Different brands have taken different public positions on it and some of them are now having to deal with the backlash it brings. Studies show that employees and customers want organizations to have a voice on issues that matter to them – as long as the companies' position is in line with their own. Fear that important stakeholders will be 'upset' by an organization's position often causes management to refuse to speak out on important issues, especially on social media.

It is social media – with Facebook and Twitter leading the way – that a large number of PR managers identify as the main cause of polarization of society (see figure *Reasons for the polarization of society* in Chapter 3). These two platforms, they say, give voice and audience to people who use disinformation to spread their political views. For example, on controversial issues such as immigration, more than half of the information disseminated on Twitter comes from untrustworthy sources.

While the reluctance of companies to embark on socially engaged campaigns in such an environment may be understandable, 85% of respondents to the USC survey attribute an ability to reduce the polarization of society to business. Business leadership on issues of social engagement is especially trusted by young people, with 96% of students agreeing that the private sector has the potential to reduce the polarization of American society. Exactly 85% of respondents also expect the number of activist brands to increase over the next five years, with 73% saying that active steps will come from their own companies and clients in the next 12 months.

Why do leaders put so much faith in brand activism? The reasons stem from the topics we've covered in this chapter. Stakeholder capitalism leads companies to believe that their role is to bring about positive social change. Second on the list is the desire to act in line with corporate values and purpose. Personal beliefs also play a significant role. Actively pursuing the values that people in the organization believe in is simply the right thing to do.

PR, a discipline whose long-standing principle has been to avoid controversy and risk, is entering a new era. Communications professionals have the opportunity to become advocates for social engagement, and this has huge implications for the future of the entire industry, not to mention the potential for corporate leadership. Well-executed brand activism can improve reputation and positively impact company performance – for example, increase sales. A great example of brand activism done well is Patagonia. It's no coincidence that when researchers at the University of Southern California asked PR professionals which company in their opinion communicated its corporate mission most effectively, this outdoor apparel brand came out on top.

The challenge for professional communicators will thus be to satisfy the desire of stakeholders to be a force for good in the world, avoiding the pitfalls that brand activism brings, while uniting, not dividing, society through their work.

Patagonia: Masterclass of Purpose-Driven Brand Activism

1. *Strong purpose*

Patagonia has a clearly stated purpose, which is *We're in the business to save our home planet.* In terms of communication, this motto is a clever blend of a perhaps brashly ambitious goal, but one that responds to the needs of customers and other stakeholders. At the same time, the company's mission is quite clearly translated into real actions that Patagonia is actually taking to protect the environment.

2. Commitment

Patagonia communicates and follows its corporate mission authentically. The brand prioritizes long-term goals over short-term results. For example, it was the first manufacturer of fleece made from recycled bottles. It began producing it in 1993, long before words like 'sustainability' and 'ecology' became today's buzzwords. Patagonia also repairs torn or otherwise damaged clothing. It has also caught the attention of professional communicators around the world with its iconic campaign *Don't buy this jacket*, in which it discourages people from purchase of its own product.

3. Authenticity

Patagonia has come to embody the values of millions of people who care about the environment and want to join the 'mission to save the planet'. The brand dedicates its human and financial capacity to activism, supports many non-profit organizations and environmental activists, and demonstrates through its actions what modern brand activism looks like.

REASONS FOR PUBLIC ENGAGEMENT

What are the primary reasons for increasing public engagement?

1	Because of commitment to positive social change	44 %
2	Because it aligns with our/their values	41 %
3	Because it is the right thing to do	36 %
4	To enhance brand reputation	33 %
5	Customer demands	23 %
6	To attract the best talent	22 %
7	Employee requests	20 %
8	Senior management priorities	17 %
9	Because other companies are getting involved	15 %
10	To increase sales	13 %
11	Activist pressure	13 %

source: 2022 Global Communication Report. USC Annenberg Center for Public Relations

ESSENTIAL STEPS HOW TO BECOME A LEADER WHILE SAVING THE WORLD

1. *Focus on comprehensive ESG measurement and implement ESG principles into your operations.* A continuous strategic effort to measure, evaluate and benchmark the impact of your business on society and the planet will strongly affect your potential for leadership. As many companies around the world are already doing so, ESG and sustainability reporting will sooner or later affect us all. It is no longer enough to focus only on CSR.

2. *If you want to succeed as a leader, you will need to explain what you believe in and how it can benefit key stakeholders – people, society, the planet and shareholders.* Your purpose will then attract those who are heading in the same direction.

3. *Use your purpose to define where your brand will be active in terms of societal issues.* Make your purpose the North Star that guides what you do and makes it easy for stakeholders to understand why you have a particular position on societal issues.

4. *Step outside your comfort zone and don't be shy about engaging in topics that address polarized views.* This is your responsibility, as social polarization is a significant risk factor for organizations.

5. *Identify where you want the brand to have an active position on societal issues.* Build this into your communications strategy to reinforce belief in your purpose. Don't be afraid to become advocates for social engagement.

7

HOW TO MAKE YOUR WORKPLACE SO INSPIRING THAT IT ATTRACTS AND RETAINS THE BEST TALENT?

Employer Branding, Diversity, Equity and Inclusion and Changing Company Culture

Almost every sector in the world, from industry to services – public relations not excluded – is facing a shortage of talent. Whether the reason is that the industry is doing tremendously well, not doing well at all, or a mass employee exodus following a pandemic, leaders face a major challenge: attracting and retaining talent despite difficult times. The role of communication is crucial. Professional communicators can help leaders significantly in their quest to become an attractive employer. Their absence, on the other hand, can cause significant difficulties for leadership.

* * * * *

IF WE KEEP LOOKING FOR TALENT IN THE SAME PLACES, WE WON'T BE ABLE TO BUILD A BETTER INDUSTRY

Rich Leigh

Even before hiring my very first employee, I knew that I couldn't hope to build a PR business alone, or without care for the people that come into the agency.

Our industry relies on the time and talent of people, and as such, that's what we sell.

Very early on, I set out to build an agency that put and continues to put people first. In fact, our company motto, which we've unofficially had in place for as long as I can recall is: 'a happy team, doing great work, WITH (not for) happy clients'.

We cannot run a successful business without a happy team, and everything we do speaks to ensuring the happiness of our team, first and foremost. It makes sense to me that, if they are happy, they will do their best work, and if they are doing their best work, clients will be happy. Of course, there's a capitalistic aspect to this that I don't ever shy away from - this emphasis reduces team and client turnover; two things that can seriously damage an agency.

I've long said to our team that we all have to work for a living. I know that I'd sooner do so in a place where people feel valued and where we can actually enjoy what we do for a living as much as possible.

Radioactive's company policies are industry-leading and have made headlines around the world, leading to us being fortunate enough to win multiple 'Best Place to Work' awards. In 2018, we became one of the first companies in the UK to adopt a four-day working week, reducing total working hours, but while still committing to five-days' pay. I've been dismissed as having done so for the headlines, but I can say hand-on-heart that I did it for all of the right reasons - and any good PR person knows there are far easier ways to generate coverage than doing something quite so bold, that could potentially affect margins and client management so badly!

Our noisy approach to team happiness works brilliantly from a recruitment perspective. We're inundated with CVs when job roles go live, and not only is staff retention high, but we've had two members of the team that left to go to other roles return – citing our culture as a real reason for wanting to.

All that said, Covid has impacted workplace culture and the employer-employee relationship forever. In the UK, although more than half of PR agencies made redundancies during the pandemic, as things have returned to a more stable footing, there is now a real and rightful understanding on the behalf of employees of their own value.

As an employer, there are a number of ways we're keen to ensure the quantity and quality of applicants stays high, and that our current team feels valued.

The actual work environment has always mattered – but now, where we have had employees working from home, there's a shift towards a hybrid model of both in-office and at-home work that I think will exist for decades to come and possibly forever.

That said, I truly do believe our best work is done together, given the creative nature of public relations, and our profit margin certainly speaks to that. I also believe that there's such a lot of osmotic learning and career development done, especially in the first few years of your PR career, so my preference is to be both forward-thinking and honest. We already had a hybrid model in place at Radioactive given the four day week, but we've decided to put a working-from-home allowance in place too, giving the team flexibility to choose when they're in, but giving us enough notice that it doesn't affect the day-to-day running of the business.

With so much competition for talent, PR employers need to walk the walk when it comes to team happiness, and really strike the balance between that and being in existence to make money.

The shift over the next couple of decades will be one that does away with empty Casual Dress Friday-style platitudes and instead embraces *the fact that our employees are human beings, and as such, financial remuneration makes up only one aspect of their decision to choose a company. Policies that speak to life outside of work, such as parental leave, adoption, bereavement, fertility treatment, health benefits, diversity and cultural considerations, charitable support and others have become just as important as salary for many, where their employer's public branding and stance is an important differentiating factor.*

Another area I think we are failing in is diversity of recruitment. If we keep looking in the same places for talent, we'll fail to build a better, more diverse industry. As such, I want our industry to delve more into pre-graduate spaces. How do we reach 16–18-year-old students, for instance, to firstly tell them that PR exists as a career choice, and secondly to bring them into it? At Radioactive, we're putting in place paid work experience during school holidays, and talking at schools and colleges to have a local impact. I believe this will help hugely when it comes to social mobility for people that might otherwise have no idea how to access a lucrative career in a creative industry. Over the next two decades, I want to see an end to reports highlighting pay differences for women, people of colour and people from lower socio-economic backgrounds and I invite other agency owners to really consider how we can achieve this.

Add those business decisions to more ethical stances, such as the types of clients and work we'd take on, and you have an industry that has had to and will continue to have to reckon with the fact that the talent market has asked for change. PR employers need to be willing to listen.

* * * * *

We cannot run a successful business without a happy team, and everything we do speaks to ensuring the happiness of our team, first and foremost.

Who Is Rich Leigh

Rich Leigh isn't afraid to break with convention and take risks, as when he once lost a bet and legally changed his name to Mr Public Relations. His passion is creative PR campaigns. In 2012, he started the multi-contributor site PRexamples.com, reaching 60,000+ PR and marketing people each month, which  soon became one of the most read PR blogs in the UK. Rich Leigh loves social media – the platform Buzzsumo named him the most influential Twitter PR person (@RichLeighPR), and he was named one of the 'the brightest young social media communicators' by the UK Social Media Communications Awards. His book PR Myths quickly became a best-selling book on Amazon. In 2014, he founded his own agency, Radioactive.

HOW TO SOLVE THE PROBLEM OF PEOPLE RETENTION AND ATTRACTION

When the term *employer branding* is mentioned, most people may think of brands that are dream job destinations for many candidates: Google, Microsoft, and Amazon are regularly ranked among the top employers. The top 10 of the Forbes annual rankings are usually occupied exclusively by technology companies.

What if you're not Jeff Bezos and your industry isn't exactly brimming with tech opportunities? Don't despair. Even if you're not one of the tech giants and don't have their fat budgets at your disposal, you can still be pretty sexy to job seekers.

Any organization that is serious about its people can be appealing in the labour market. That is the message of the article written by Rich Leigh for this book. His agency, Radioactive, is a shining example that, with the right commitment, you can create a truly stimulating, creative and enticing environment and achieve successes as an employer that you never dreamed possible. Rich's perspective in his text may be agency-based, but most of the principles he writes about can be applied anywhere.

'Just' follow the simple rule that Rich Leigh repeats several times in the text: *people come first, because your potential for leadership is directly proportional to the amount of talent you can concentrate in your team.* I put the word 'just' in quotes for a simple reason – keeping your company on track is no easy feat in employer branding. It takes trust in people and in your intuition, and above all the courage to go against the tide when needed – the qualities of a true leader.

In most surveys that look at the top challenges of a given industry – whether it's PR or any other industry – talent acquisition or retention comes up high on the list. After all, Crispin Manners reflects on the same topic in his text in Chapter 6. The Worldcom Confidence Index (an AI-powered survey to track global business confidence and trends that Crispin and I co-invented for the Worldcom PR Group) shows that the approach to talent retention is changing in response to societal and technological developments. For example, e.g. Index data suggests a trend that leaders might focus on retaining only those employees who believe in the purpose of the organization and who embrace a new way of operating.[1]

Talent management and employer branding are therefore both a challenge and an opportunity for communications professionals.

It's a challenge because the challenges we face are significant. To be able to implement everything written in this book and be leaders in the future, we need highly educated and motivated people with open minds, ready to develop.

The opportunity lies in being able to create campaigns that will reduce turnover or increase the interest of candidates in the particular industry or employers. This fits right in with the concept of delivering campaigns that have a real impact on the organization (as we have discussed in Chapter 5).

Building an employer brand is a long haul that needs professional communicators to keep it on track. They are the ones who

---

[1] *Worldcom Confidence Index Global Results.* (January 2022) Worldcom Public Relations Group.

can accurately capture, name, and communicate your company's uniqueness, and therefore deliver measurable results.

A CASE STUDY: MOTOROLA

The story of Motorola is a case in point. This technology company, whose service centre in Brno, Czechia – a shared service centre for about half the world –, produces integrated electrical circuits, mobile phones, terminals, processors and other devices. The employee base of the service centre in the Moravian capital is very diverse – blue-collar, professions, administrative staff and managers of different nationalities work in the same building and meet every day. Nevertheless, the general opinion among Brno residents was that the Motorola service centre was a 'factory'. In the labour market, this led to the mistaken assumption that possible employment at Motorola in Brno was not attractive for capable, educated and ambitious candidates. The situation called for a repositioning of the employer brand.

The communication campaign, prepared by my agency PRAM Consulting, focused primarily on improving internal communication, correcting the distorted public image and reputation of the company, and increasing the attractiveness of the brand for existing and potential employees.

The internal communication needed to ensure that employees understood the nature and importance of their colleagues' work and that they were familiar with the company's values and culture. The communication was also aimed at making them aware that there was no need to make distinctions between different positions or nationalities of team members, but that a diverse cultural background can instead be very enriching and contribute to a common goal. The campaign therefore focused mainly on promoting team building activities that spanned all teams. For example, we organized a joint barbecue for employees and their families, where they enjoyed regional European specialities and played games that delivered experiences from different cultures. Shared experiences bring people together.

As part of our external communication, we started by raising awareness about working at the company and informed about employee benefits such as an international environment with personal development opportunities, the chance to gain experience abroad and attractive pay. By working with local universities, we were able to introduce the campaign to graduates and reached the public through regional media. To strengthen the brand, Motorola held a series of Open Days and internal seminars to explain its purpose.

Through our efforts, we were able to reduce annual employee turnover by 50%. Then, in an internal survey, most employees said they better understood the meaning and importance of their colleagues' work. In addition, employees became brand ambassadors and began to spontaneously spread the company's good name. As a result, the number of new applicants for the service centre was three times higher after the campaign than at the beginning.

While you always need to tailor employer branding to a specific company, there are a few rules you can follow.

HOW TO MAKE YOUR EMPLOYER BRAND DRIVE RETENTION AND ATTRACTION

1. Ask your employees what makes a perfect future colleague

Are you asking employees for their opinion? If not, you should start. By involving your team in the hiring process, you'll avoid mistakes that can ultimately cost your company money. Involving employees in the hiring decision-making process is on the rise for companies, but this entire strategy must go hand-in-hand with effective internal communication. Existing employees need to be reassured that they are important to the company, communicating the positives that their work brings them as well as current events in the company. Then your team itself will spread the company's good name among other potential employees, as happened in the case of Motorola.

2. Let others spread the word about the company

You can't rely on what *you* say about the company, i.e. your image, to build a strong employer brand. For truly effective employer branding, you need a good reputation. Data from CareerArc says that up to 68% of millennials purposefully follow potential employers on social media. Invest in new digital communication channels and build your image as a great place to work through dialogue, not monologue. Employee ambassadors can also help you do this, and their activity on the networks – as long as it sheds a positive light on your company, of course – is essential. This reinforces the need to be a people first organization so that employee comments are positive.

3. *Don't try to please everyone. Make sure you attract employees who believe in your purpose and like your company culture*

Careful communication will attract the right employees, i.e., ones who will believe in your purpose and like your company culture. Reaching out to candidates who aren't a good fit for a job at your company is a waste of time. Not to mention the hassle of recruiting such a candidate. That's why it's important to know what it means to work in your company, or for a specific position, to have a successful recruitment campaign. If you are not sure, listen to your employees and present yourself in their words. This honesty will significantly increase the chances that you will reach candidates who will enjoy working for you, feel comfortable in your company's environment, and will further develop the work environment. The result will be much less employee turnover.

4. *Engage potential employees with authentic (video) content*

The popular mantra of marketers that the human ability to hold attention has been reduced to just eight seconds is not entirely based on truth (nor is the claim that consumers are like goldfish – even goldfish can hold attention for more than a few seconds).[2] The data comes from a relatively small study, and there is evidence that our attention span varies depending on what we pay attention to. But if anything changes, it's our preferences and demands for content. In this regard, video is growing in importance, making it an increasingly popular format for employer branding campaigns. Just remember that you don't want to test the attention of potential employees for long – the video should grab their attention in the first few seconds, feel authentic and the

---

[2]Maybin, B. S. (2017) Busting the attention span myth. Available at: https://www.bbc.com/news/health-38896790.

information in it should be up-to-date and go hand-in-hand with the content you're presenting on your website and social media.

5. Engage your customers – make them your brand ambassadors

All the tips so far have focused on employees, but when it comes to describing your brand, customers have something to say too. After all, it is your customer who is in regular contact with your employees and who can evaluate their behaviour. So, when gathering information and opinions about your company, be sure to ask your clients as well, as this is also how you can reach out to new potential team members.

6. Don't get left behind in employer branding

75% of active job seekers are more likely to respond to an advertisement from a company that actively nurtures its employer brand. And 86% of employees and job seekers consider company reviews and ratings when deciding where to apply for a job. These two telling statistics clearly show why caring about your company's reputation as an employer is important to future leaders. In a world where finding the right talent is a key ingredient for success, it pays to have the right PR and employer branding strategy to bear fruit.

* * * * *

DIVERSITY, EQUITY AND INCLUSION BRING A PARADIGM SHIFT

Imma Folch-Lázaro

The future needs to be diverse and inclusive, and communicators the change agents.

Incorporating diversity and inclusion into business strategy produces benefits. These benefits have already been measured by hundreds of studies; we don't need to take a leap of faith. Applying a diversity and inclusion lens is not just cool or trendy; it is a paradigm shift. Companies that incorporate diversity and inclusion into all of their policies and processes are more innovative, earn higher profits, have more resilient and empowered work teams, greater brand recognition, and most importantly, attract more talent.

According to Mckinsey&Company 2018 Report 'Delivering through Diversity' companies in the top-quartile for **gender diversity** on executive teams were 21% more likely to outperform their national industry median on Earnings Before Interest and Taxes (EBIT) margin and 27% on EP margin.[3]

Companies with the most **ethnically/culturally** diverse boards worldwide are 43% more likely to experience higher profits. Diversity brings to the table different experiences, views, and managing problems, thus fuelling innovation, which represents higher profits.

Today, a large percentage of the workforce belongs to the 'millennial' and 'Z' generations. In the future, the market will be theirs. Millennials and Gen-Z are looking for jobs in line with their values, companies that promote social justice and sustainability. Today and in the future, they will be loyal to companies that have a purpose with which they identify.

'86% of female and 74% of male millennials say an employer's policy on diversity, equality, and workforce inclusion is important to them when deciding whether or not to work for an organisation', finds PriceWaterhouse in their 2019 research 'The female millennial. A new area of talent'.[4] If you don't have a policy on DEI you will missing the checklist of 7 out of 10 of potential talent. And that's a clear disadvantage for the future success of your organization. Furthermore, American Express and Kantar Futures, found that 74% of millennials define the successful businesses of the future as those who 'have a genuine purpose that resonates with people'.[5] Success will be measured in terms of people belonging on the long term much more than on sales in the short term.

But there is no universal recipe for moving towards a diverse, equitable and inclusive organization. Let's start because every culture looks at diversity through a different lens. What works in one country, market, or industry may not resonate in others and may even have the opposite effect. Each culture has its own wounds and legacies, and

---

[3]Hunt. V., Yee, L., Prince, S. & Dixon-Fyle, S. (2018) *Delivering through diversity.*
[4]PwC 2019. *The female millennial: A new area of talent.*
[5]American Express/Kantar Futures: *Business The millenial way.*

power groups differ across markets and industries. Take time to understand how different diversities are expressed, and understand the local agents of change. Collaborating with local agencies is more important than ever, especially for organizations that span multiple markets.

People in leadership positions are responsible for initiating change towards an inclusive future. Without their involvement, account-ability is diluted, and progress slows. And this is a big challenge for the leader, even for those with transactional or servant leadership, as he or she must confront his or her own beliefs and biases. It involves being open to ones own personal change and breaking through internal and rooted resistances. The leader has to combine a transformative and inclusive mindset with concrete actions to bring change in organiza-tions. The leader has to embrace a courageous leadership and drive change management to become more inclusive and diverse.

The courageous leader will be those who thrive in the feature. What defines a courageous leader? Matt Gavin, in his article for Harvard Business School '5 Characteristics of a Courageous Leader' define them as authenticity, resilience, with a high degree of emotional intelligence, self-discipline, and commitment to purpose.[6] All of them require a breakthrough and personal work.

Perhaps in the future we will see younger leaders, as they are more willing to break the status quo by being true to their own values and lead with passion and purpose.

Communication agencies have to be the first to drive change by looking into our own organizations. It's not enough to have diverse teams, that's just a pretty picture. We must be intentional and put diversity to work, to have a real impact on us and on our clients. How do we do that?

Let's start by reviewing all the tools we use, let's reset and adapt the way we work to the diverse and inclusive world we aspire to create. We must go beyond our own experiences, accumulated over the years, learn by listening, and discover our own unconscious biases, both as organizations and as individuals. From there, let us promote inclusive language, both written and visual, let us seek gender parity in spokespersons, diverse representation of our customers, let us develop

---

[6]Gavin, Matt. (2020) '5 characteristics of a courageous leader'.

communication strategies that include all audiences, let us seek the social and sustainable impact of conscious communication. Our teams must show their true selves and connect with the true selves of our clients.

If organizations incorporate diversity and inclusion into their business strategies, the diversity and inclusion communication strategy must be aligned with corporate communication. Developing a diversity and inclusion communication plan starts with defining its position in the organization, and companies of the future will need to include it in their overall communication plans, both in external and internal communication.

Metrics must also change. If something matters, it must be measured, and if it is measured, it is because it matters. Today we use metrics to measure the results of actions, but diversity and inclusion require metrics of intent and engagement as well. To be effective, metrics must align with outcomes that produce systemic change. We know how to measure what we produce – content –, how we distribute it – channels, tools –, but we must also measure impact – changes in behaviour, actions taken by audiences. what should we measure to see the effectiveness of the diversity and inclusion communication strategy? We will measure what answers the question 'what do we want to achieve with our strategy?'

Institutions and communications professionals in particular must assume the role of guarantors of truth. Real news, not manipulated by algorithms or commercial interests, is a surefire way to stay on track and keep us focussed on inequality. The future brings us personalization, which could pose a threat to inclusivity. If we are not exposed to these differences, it is difficult for us to understand them and therefore accept them, because people tend to be afraid of what they do not understand. Now more than ever, as communications professionals, we must play a key role in driving diversity and inclusion into our clients' communications strategies. If we've learned anything from organizations and ourselves over the past few years, it's that the only constant is change, and the resilience we need to keep in constant motion comes from our values.

Incorporating diversity and inclusion as a core value and inherent in a purpose that resonates with society will enable us to strengthen our resilience as individuals and as organizations to face a changing future.

* * * * *

> If you don't have a policy on DEI you will missing the checklist of 7 out of 10 of potential talent. And that's a clear disadvantage for the future success of your organization.

Who Is Imma Folch-Lázaro

It would be hard to find someone more experienced in communication of diversity, equity and inclusion than Imma Folch-Lázaro. She is Diversity, Equity and Inclusion Chair of Worldcom PR Group EMEA, CEO and founder of LF Channel PR agency and a co-founder of the Diversity, Equity and Inclusion consulting firm, Bein Mindset s.l. Over the past 25 years, Imma have helped more than 500 companies to increase their visibility and market share through communication and marketing programs. She is committed to generate positive changes in society and a strong believer that life is 10% what happens to you and 90% what you do with it.

THE GROWING IMPORTANCE OF DEI

When you say *diversity and inclusion*, a memory comes to mind that happened years ago. Back then, I went to the United States where one of my friends gave me the opportunity to work for a few months in a larger American PR agency. I had never worked in a corporate-type agency before, let alone abroad, so I was very curious to see how things were in the 'big world' overseas.

I was not disappointed. I gained new and valuable experience regarding company culture, processes and service. I also noticed one thing – the agency was staffed primarily by white Americans, with a minority of Hispanics and Asians, but no African Americans. As an outsider, I found that strange, so one day at lunch I asked about this disparity. My colleague replied that it was the bane of the PR industry. African Americans are usually smart, driven and ambitious and the 'poor industry that is PR' simply doesn't attract them. When they do choose to work in communications, they are more likely to go into advertising, public affairs or digital communications. These are places where higher budgets are concentrated and thus bring a greater chance of financial success.

This story took place shortly after the crisis in 2009 and it must be said that the agency from this story is currently leading the way in diversity and inclusion. However, the story points to two PR problems.

- Public relations struggles with a lack of diversity

- Public relations often fails to attract young talent, potential leaders, and especially members of minority groups

UNDERSTANDING DIVERSITY (PROBLEM) IN PR

If we as PR professionals care about the future of our industry, the limping of PR in diversity, equity and inclusion (abbreviated DEI) should make us wince – as Imma Folch-Lázaro writes in her prediction, applying DEI is not just cool or fashionable, it is a paradigm shift.

What is diversity anyway? The term encompasses all the ways in which people – groups and individuals – differ from one another. Although diversity is often thought of in terms of race, ethnicity and gender, there are other, much broader elements of diversity. These include age, nationality, religion, disability, sexual orientation, socio-economic status, education, marital status, language and physical appearance.

However, even the basic parameters of diversity are not very positive for our industry. According to data from the US Bureau of

Labor Statistics, the ethnic makeup of PR managers in the US looks like this: more than 89% are white, 7.2% are Hispanic, 4.4% are Asian, 3.5% are African American. Among PR specialists, nearly 83.7% are white, 12.1% are Hispanic, 4.5% are Asian and 8.9% are African American.[7]

The situation is not much better for our female colleagues either. The latest data from Global Women in PR shows that while two-thirds of our industry's workforce is female, when it comes to corporate leadership and senior management, the ratio turns against women – 66% of positions are held by men.[8]

Moreover, it is important to remember that even if the numbers become more equal, we are far from winning. It is not for nothing that discussions on diversity add in the same breath that equity and inclusion are also needed. Equity means fair treatment, access, opportunity and advancement for all people. One of the most pressing equity issues is, of course, fair pay – or the lack of it in the form of the pay gap.

The pay gap in public relations manifests itself both between men and women and, perhaps even more significantly, between members of the white majority and the non-white minority. To give you an idea, the Holmes Report in 2017 came up with the following numbers: compared to white men, white women in PR earn about $6,000 less per year, non-white men about $9,000 less, and non-white women as much as $15,000 less. Of course, the numbers vary from company to company, state to state, and change over time, but what hasn't changed is the fact that PR has distinct problems in the areas of diversity and equity.

REASONS TO INCLUDE INCLUSION

In her article for Harvard Business Review, Angela Chitkara mentions her research in which she subjected 18 CEOs of influential PR firms (all from the top 100 of PRovoke Media's rankings) to questions on diversity and inclusion. It turns out that most of these

[7]Bureau of Labor Statistics. (2021) *Labor Force Statistics from the Current Population Survey*. US Department of Labor.
[8]Global women in PR and Opinium Research. (2021) *Global Women in PR Annual Index 2021*.

top executives conflate the two concepts into one. Only six of the CEOs interviewed commented separately on the topic of inclusion.

Without inclusion, diversity is a statistical, box-ticking exercise that has no chance of making a real difference. As Imma writes in her prediction, 'it's not enough to have diverse teams, that's just a pretty picture. We must be intentional and put diversity to work'. That is the task of equity and inclusion. They ensure that the company is not only diverse, but that everyone feels genuinely comfortable, that everyone's voices are respected, and that everyone is free to express themselves and participate fully. Lynn Casey, CEO of Padilla, put it perfectly when she said that inclusivity is, in her opinion, 'where the rubber meets the road, not only checking the box and getting x people of colour, but also making them feel welcome and making sure we understand and celebrate each other'. Kearie Daniel, Director of Public Engagement and Government Relations at Eva's, emphasizes the equity part: 'You can have an organization that is diverse and full of Black, Brown, queer or trans people... it'll look great on your website, but having diversity and including people at the table, doesn't mean there is equity. If Black people in your organization don't feel they can speak up about racism because they will be sidelined, or they will experience passive aggression, or they'll be left out of meetings or decision making, then your organization isn't equitable and all the diversity and inclusion in the world won't make it so'.

HOW TO MAKE DIVERSITY, EQUITY AND INCLUSION WORK

So how do we approach diversity, equity and inclusion? First of all, it is important to understand that diversity and inclusion is not a 'problem' that you 'solve'. As with ESG, it is a long-term and continuous process that needs to be trusted and approached with seriousness and commitment. Imma Folch-Lázaro captured the principles of a successful DEI strategy perfectly in her text. Let's summarise and generalise her principles.

1. *The foundation of an authentic organization that is guided by the principles of diversity, equity and inclusion is education* and

recognition of the biases that can hold us back on the DEI journey. Invest in training and mentoring – this applies to both staff and senior management. Revise your processes and tools in light of new knowledge and experience.

2. *Diversity, equity and inclusion should ideally become part of your purpose.* The DEI strategy should therefore be aligned with your overall communication strategy. Ensure that diversity, equity and inclusion permeate all forms of communication – internal, external, social media, leadership and visual communications.

3. *Set the goals you want to achieve in DEI.* According to these goals, set the measurement method. Remember, everything that is important, you should measure! For example, without measurement, you won't be able to determine minority employee turnover, which is one of the basic parameters of DEI, or track your progress. The data will also be useful later – for example, when creating non-financial reporting (see Chapter 6).

Going down the DEI route is worthwhile. I am personally convinced that both diversity and inclusion are opportunities for public relations to take an existential shift (see Chapter 8) in three ways.

Firstly, PR can, as is the case in ESG, show its potential and expertise on the topics of diversity and inclusion. As experts in internal and external communication, we can set and communicate a company's DEI strategy while avoiding communication misunderstandings and fails. Diversity and inclusion are therefore opportunities for new business.

Secondly, if we can improve the situation in public relations and create a truly diverse and inclusive environment within our industry, this will reflect positively on the quality of our work, its added value and the level of our campaigns. It is only by making diversity and inclusion a full part of our industry that we will be able to better understand our clients and target groups, our campaigns will be more successful and the value that PR brings will rise.

This is closely related to the third area, which is also the topic of this chapter. Diversity and inclusion will help you attract talent. Because DEI has the potential to increase the value that PR brings, the industry can generate more money. This is a chance to shed the label of 'poor industry', as an American colleague of mine once described public relations, and attract young talent. Moreover, it turns out that companies that are diverse and promote inclusion tend to have happier employees and lower turnover. Let's don't forget that happiness and well-being is the mantra of the millennials and emerging Gen-Z. Needless to say, low turnover saves significant costs.

USEFUL TOOLS TO AVOID COMMUNICATION FAILS

Examples from around the world show what happens when professional communicators turn their backs on DEI principles. For example, as when the fashion chain H&M came up with an advert showing a young black boy wearing a green hoodie and the words 'coolest monkey in the jungle'. Or when Dove ran an ad showing a dark-skinned woman gradually turning into a white woman. Or when Heineken came up with the slogan 'Sometimes, lighter is better'.

These missteps are, of course, unfortunate and can cause damage to brands that will cost a huge amount of effort and even bigger amount of money to recover from. The only real prevention is embedding DEI principles into our minds, hearts, teams and organizations. There are many practical tools for doing this. Researchers Regina Luttrell and Adrienne Wallace, for example, have invented a *Diversity and Inclusion Wheel for PR Practitioners* to help you devise inclusive campaigns from the outset.

The *Diversity and Inclusion Wheel for PR Practitioners* has at its centre six key areas that communicators should consider when starting to develop a campaign: nationality, age, physical characteristics/abilities, gender, race and ethnicity. These areas should also be considered when creating a campaign team. A homogeneous team is unlikely to come up with a diverse and inclusive campaign. The outer perimeter of the wheel then includes 17 other attributes, from marital status to religious beliefs, from communication styles to mental health and wellbeing.

Don't turn a blind eye to diversity and inclusion. It may be that when we open them up, not only will the talent be gone, but so will the profits, investor interest and our chances for leadership.

DIVERSITY & INCLUSION WHEEL
FOR PR PRACTITIONERS

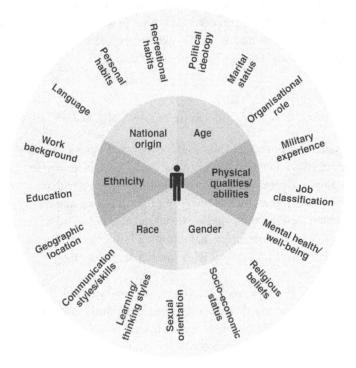

SOURCE: © R. Luttrell, A. Wallace

* * * * *

WE MUST OFFER THE BEST CAREER DEVELOPMENT AND INSPIRING LEADERSHIP

Alex Aiken

Perceived purpose in the workplace will become evermore critical to organisational success. In my case public service communication offers a powerful motivation to colleagues to work to deliver for their fellow citizen and wider society. This fundamental truth about government communication has been demonstrated in recent years by the response of communicators to the Covid crisis and recently to the tragic events in Ukraine. In both areas timely, relevant, formative public information has helped as a force for good.

Noble intentions and goals are a vitally important part of our offer, but we must also strive to make workplaces inspiring in other ways. I've recently completed professional courses on data science and contract management, and I strongly believe that as the world continues to develop at a frightening pace our ability to offer the best professional development and training is a central part of recruiting and retaining the best people, and 'future proof' their careers.

Purpose and training are of course important but leadership and good management are the other things that will make people thrive in the workplace of the future. The UK civil service asks leaders to be inspiring, confident and empowering. This is a good guide to leadership anywhere and provides us with a clear framework to lead our colleagues.

Every year our staff surveys allow us to reflect on whether our management, in terms of developing people, improving their performance and making the workplace an inclusive one, has been successful. So, in that sense, metrics tell us about whether managers are really, and empirically, improving our hybrid offices. Data remains an essential foundation for good management today and into the future.

*****

Noble intentions and goals are a vitally important part of our offer, but we must also strive to make workplaces inspiring in other ways.

Who Is Alex Aiken

Alex Aiken delivered significant change to the practice of public service communication and transformed teams in central and local government, leading policy and communication functions. He currently serves as Executive Director for the UK's Government Communication Service (GCS), which he created in 2014 and developed its campaigns approach and the Modern Communication Operating Model. He is former Director of Communications & Strategy for Westminster City Council. Alex Aiken is passionate about family, football, cricket and great communications work.

SHOW PEOPLE YOU CARE ABOUT THEIR FUTURE

Alex Aiken is right. To truly attract and retain the best talent and create a work environment that makes our employees happy, we need to know the data and the information that comes from it – about our company, the job market and societal trends in general.

Let's take a look at the latest Global Talent Trends report, which is prepared annually by LinkedIn.[9] One thing is clear: Company culture is at a turning point. The reverberating pandemic, accelerating automation, the rise of millennials and Gen-Z, and the 'Great Reshuffle' or mass exodus of employees coming in 2021 are all transformative influences.

---

[9]LinkedIn Global Talent Trends 2022 (2022) *The Reinvention of Company Culture*. LinkedIn Talent Solutions.

PLAN FOR A PEOPLE FIRST COMPANY CULTURE

The new human-centric company culture has typical characteristics: it is flexible, asynchronous (goodbye to endless live online meetings where workers from several time zones meet at the same time), emphasises trust, belonging and a holistic concept of work well-being. Work-life balance has settled at the top of the priorities. 63% of professionals put it first when choosing a new job. As a result, work-life balance surpassed even compensation and other benefits in importance (a priority for 60% of candidates).

So how to improve company culture? In the words of Alex Aiken, given the speed and unpredictability of the world, it is increasingly important to *offer personal development and education to your employees*. This topic also ranked first in the LinkedIn survey. It was identified by 59% of respondents as an area to invest in to improve company culture.

Flexibility is becoming another essential part of a company's offer to candidates. The same working hours for everyone is gone. It turns out that one-size-fits-all is a thing of the past, at least in the job market. Employees want flexibility in when, where and how they work.

Personally, I believe this is much more of an opportunity than a challenge for PR professionals. The essence of our industry has never been (and should never be) sitting 'from-to' in an office, but creativity, expertise and commitment. In this respect, we can be a truly attractive industry for talent, one that understands all too well that it's the quality of the work done, not the time served, that counts.

The challenge then for all employers is to create a working environment that meets the demands for flexibility. There is also the question of how to deal with junior staff, who are undergoing, in Rich Leigh's words, 'intense osmotic learning and career development'. But the biggest challenge, in my view, will be overcoming one's own bias. Managers must learn to look at performance metrics other than the – hitherto common – valuation of 'commitment' based on permanent presence in the office. 'Companies will start to focus on measuring results, not activities, which will be an important part of the change in corporate culture', explains Nickle LaMoreaux, who is in charge of human resources at IBM. This is essentially the same type of change I describe a few paragraphs above – the emphasis on results, not activities, will translate into the work of communications professionals everywhere.

PLAN FOR WORK LIFE BALANCE

Well-being, happiness, work-life balance. These are qualities that recruiters of the future must learn well. According to a LinkedIn study, they will be increasingly in demand on the job market. No wonder. The health of an organization is closely linked to the healthy work habits of its employees. What is expected of employers? Apart from the aforementioned flexibility, above all a human approach. This far surpasses a medical allowance or morning yoga.

For many agencies and in-house communications teams, it can be more challenging than it seems. Richard Bagnall describes the reasons brilliantly in Chapter 5 – communications teams are facing pressures that are forcing them to do more and more work with less and less money and time. Short deadlines, the fast pace and public nature of our profession, the fickle human factor, the emphasis on creativity, originality and return on investment… As a result, PR ranks among the 10 most stressful careers to choose, along with other positions in communications and journalism, according to CareerCast.com. Only professional soldiers, firefighters, pilots and police officers beat us. Event organizers also ranked higher, but this is a job that many PR specialists know and do.

I don't think a four-day work week will fix that. While this approach certainly doesn't hurt and will give communications professionals more time to recover and rest on the weekend, the stress is unlikely to go away. The causes of the stressfulness of our jobs run deeper.

Let's use PR agencies to demonstrate the need for certain rules and structure. Most agencies were founded by highly creative people who are great communicators and marketers. Despite the fact that the vast majority of PR professionals can produce a press release, manage crisis communications or prepare social media campaigns with ease, when it comes to professionalizing their own companies and their processes, PR is often falling behind. Few agencies have clearly outlined internal processes around the responsibilities of individual roles in the team, the long-term training of people or the quality control of work. This disorderly bohemian approach may work for some, but it only works up to a point. I firmly believe that if a company sets and describes clear rules for its operations, responsibilities and procedures, every employee will be relieved of at least half of the stress. This is because rules help people identify paths and find the right solutions, and the absence of rules puts the pressure of decision-making on the individual. It doesn't have to be that way.

I therefore discuss the principles of quality management in detail in Chapter 9. In addition to the above, it is also related to the trends described in the LinkedIn study. If the future belongs to hybrid offices, how do we train a new colleague in matters related to both PR practice and the culture of our organizations? Forcing the poor newcomer to go to the office every day while colleagues enjoy their home office is not the solution. The future of how organizations operate brings with it the need to set up processes to reflect different styles of working (from home, from the office or even from the train). A well-planned and thoughtful onboarding process will ensure that the newcomer is on par with the other team members in terms of knowledge, without requiring them to be in the office more often. This example can be applied to any part of our work, whether it's knowledge of company strategy, financial management, account management and more.

USE THE GREAT RESHUFFLE AS AN OPPORTUNITY

The last massive trend that LinkedIn mentions is the large exodus of employees that occurred after the pandemic. LinkedIn optimistically calls it the 'Great Reshuffle'. And indeed, it was great: according to the Microsoft Work Trend Index, a whopping 41% of employees in 2021 said they were considering leaving their jobs in the next 12 months. This was definitely not idle talk. Labour shortages are hampering industries around the world, from China to the United States, where a record 4.3 million workers quit in August 2021 alone.[10]

Public relations has not escaped the battle for talent, of course. Anyone who wants to be a leader, in any industry, will need to focus on building a strong and attractive company culture, which is an increasingly important value for the next generation of employees. Ryan Roslansky, CEO of LinkedIn, comments: 'Business leaders are rethinking their entire working models, cultures, and company values. Employees are rethinking not just how they work, but why'. On the road to success, therefore, companies cannot do without an authentic and compelling purpose (see Chapter 6), from which corporate culture organically emerges. All areas of 'doing good' are becoming increasingly important. ESG, CSR and brand activism can be a great reason for potential and existing employees to work for a company. Thus, by taking conscious steps in the areas of sustainability, diversity and engagement in social issues, an organization dramatically increases its chances of attracting and retaining talent.

That's why, the Great Reshuffle presents a great opportunity for us communicators. Employer branding will be more important than ever. Those who get it and let potential employees know about themselves first will gain a huge advantage in leadership. Being seen and heard will be key. Candidates are getting pickier: they viewed almost twice as many websites when looking for a job in 2021 than in 2019. But with professional employer branding, companies can reach the right candidates with an authentic purpose-driven message.

While candidates may be picky and demanding, companies can't do without fresh talent. Moreover, as seen in the following chapter, it is the digital natives of the emerging Gen-Z who can contribute their knowledge of technology, and the world as seen through screens, to make our organizations truly future-ready.

---

[10]Bureau of Labor Statistics. (2021) *Quits rate of 2.9 percent in August 2021 an all-time high*. US Department of Labor.

ESSENTIAL STEPS TO ATTRACTING AND RETAINING THE BEST TALENTS

1. *Don't limit where you look for talent.* Looking for talent in the traditional places is unlikely to bring the diversity of skills needed to succeed in the future. So, create a picture of the future skills you need and develop a career path that develops these skills from within and attracts them from outside.

2. *Set up quality management processes to help new and existing employees know their possibilities and responsibilities.* By setting up processes that people in the company can follow, you help make working less stressful.

3. *Offer your employees the best personal development and education as a core part of your company's strategy.* After all, the most important part of your organization is neither business nor profit, but people.

4. *Plan for a future that includes a flexible working model.* It is therefore essential to meet the needs of people who expect flexibility and to think about how to take this model into account in onboarding and training for junior positions.

5. *In the highly competitive talent recruitment landscape, you should live up to your promises regarding team happiness.* The key is to strike a precise balance between employee satisfaction and the fact that at the end of the day, the organization needs to achieve its goals.

6. *Take DEI principles into account when developing communication campaigns.* Diversity, equity, and inclusion will help you create campaigns that are understandable and attractive to all. Be aware that a brainstorming session consisting of 10 middle-aged married white men is unlikely to yield a ground-breaking and creative idea.

8

HOW WILL AI CHANGE YOUR POTENTIAL FOR LEADERSHIP?

The Role of Technology in Communication

In the future, how will technology shape what communications professionals do? Will we still go for coffee with a journalist and discuss possible topics for publication? Or will a smart app using big data show us what a particular journalist will write about? The communications profession is currently facing a period of unrivalled disruption. How do we prepare to deliver more value alongside those changes?

* * * * *

ROGER HURNI

AI Will Affect Many Areas of Journalism

The future of journalism is a bit of a moving target. But we do know one thing for certain, artificial intelligence (AI) is going to factor into many aspects. This of course will include research, but it could find its way into story development, search engine optimization, and even automated writing.

This will have a profound effect on how leaders of organizations need to act and respond to this dynamic new world of journalism and public relations (PR). At the heart of this will be a behaviour centric model of journalism.

This behaviour centric approach will factor into the actions associated by organizations, their partners, their vendors and most importantly, their customers. Because AI will be at the core of journalistic endeavours, every algorithm will have to factor in both implicit as well as explicit behaviours associated with any given topic. This is accomplished by factoring in the motivations behind any behaviour, how easily that behaviour is achieved, and what has prompted the behaviour. This can effectively allow the algorithm to do predictive analysis on future behaviours based on the content it's providing the end-user.

For example, a journalist may need to craft a story on the effects of food processing as it pertains to population growth. A behaviour-based AI would be able to examine the diet and food purchasing of a population on a scale that the journalist simply couldn't. While this would certainly create richer content for the article, that same AI algorithm could also provide the journalist with different sets of outcome models based on the behaviour changes it would predict.

Something this simple can add an entirely new dimension to an article. In turn, the Chief Executive Officer (CEO) of a food manufacturing company would have to react in new ways to deal with the line of questioning a journalist would ask in an interview. Leaders that aren't prepared for that dynamic would find themselves in difficult situations.

* * * * *

Because AI will be at the core of journalistic endeavours, every algorithm will have to factor in both implicit as well as explicit behaviours associated with any given topic.

Who Is Roger Hurni

Roger Hurni, founder and partner of Off Madison Ave, brings a unique perspective as a behaviour strategist, creative professional, and branding expert. With a background that spans regional, national and international clientele, Roger's focus is on behavioural marketing. He helps brands achieve unprecedented results by optimizing the variables of consumer behaviour. This allows him to develop the strategic marketing initiatives necessary for companies to realize new levels of customer personalization and marketing effectiveness.

Embrace the Right Technological Tools in Public Relations

When we talk about the future, most of us think of a world where modern technology is much more prominent. The concept of artificial intelligence no longer shocks anyone, and if it does, the most they'll wonder is why your organization isn't already using it. Neural networks and smart algorithms have subtly and irreversibly become part of our lives and communications hasn't been left behind.

AI takes part in journalism and PR in different ways and at different stages of activities. The example outlined by Roger Hurni is one possibility. It illustrates that change facilitated by technology is inevitable. In 10 years time, most of us will be doing a different job, and if not, we will be doing our current job in a significantly different way.

The first area of journalism and PR that is greatly influenced by modern technology, apps and artificial intelligence is article preparation. We already rely much more heavily on search engine algorithms to research and prepare topics and to find out what people are searching for online and what topics are trending – the Google Trends platform is a typical example.

Data, the backbone of any good article, is largely available online (most public authorities, such as Eurostat or national statistical offices, publish it regularly) and data journalists are no longer a new and rare profession. Their work helps to extract new information from available data, and the future is unlikely to change the importance of data journalism much. On the contrary, the influx of data that we will have to (and, above all, want to) deal with will continue to grow. The data analyst will therefore be one of the most important people in the company – these 'data experts' are already employed by many media houses. Successful leadership has and will require constant sorting and evaluation of available data, across all phases of communications, marketing and business.

The next phase of journalistic work, content creation, has already been transformed by technology with the advent of data-driven storytelling, which we explored in Chapter 4. The burning question is whether AI can automatically generate articles in the future. The short answer is: probably yes. As long as the texts have a genre and source data, a machine can write most of them. For example, an app named Quartz has been running as a chatbot since 2012, offering global economic and political news in the Facebook Messenger environment. The Heliograph software, which has been used by the Washington Post for several years, can automatically generate articles, and in 2020 the newspaper even deployed it on its podcast channel, where it read news from the presidential election vote count in the voice of artificial intelligence.

Nowadays, we can try to develop a content with ChatGPT (Generative Pre- Trained Transformer), which is an autoregressive language model that uses deep learning to produce human-like text developed by OpenAI.

It is mind-blowing how an app is able to develop content in such a short time and such a quality. In purpose for this book I did short interview with ChatGPT about future of PR industry. Here is what exactly I got from it:

Me: What are the main challenges of public relations
           industry in the future:

ChatGPT: There are several challenges facing the public relations
           industry in the future, including:

1. Managing the impact of social media: With the rise of social media, traditional PR strategies may no longer be effective, and organizations must find ways to manage the online conversation and protect their reputation.

2. Maintaining transparency and trust: As consumers become more sceptical of corporations and government agencies, PR professionals will need to find new ways to build and maintain trust with their audiences.

3. Adapting to changing technology: New technologies, such as artificial intelligence and augmented reality, are transforming the way organizations communicate and interact with their audiences. PR professionals will need to stay up-to-date with these developments and understand how they can be used to reach new audiences.

4. Balancing short-term results with long-term strategies: The pressure to deliver quick results can lead organizations to focus on short-term initiatives rather than developing long-term strategies. PR professionals will need to find ways to balance these competing demands and create integrated programs that achieve both short-term and long-term goals.

Meeting the demands of a globalized world: As the world becomes more interconnected, PR professionals must be able to navigate complex cultural differences and address global issues in a way that is culturally sensitive and effective.

Me: I am writing book about future of Public Relations industry, which includes also usage of different application, big data, machine learning and AI. What do you think about usage of big data, machine learning and AI?

ChatGPT: The usage of big data, machine learning, and AI can bring many opportunities for the future of the Public Relations industry. Here are a few benefits:

1. Improved Targeting: With the help of big data, PR professionals can gain insights into consumer behaviour and preferences, enabling them to target their campaigns and messages more effectively.

2. Automation of Routine Tasks: Machine learning and AI can automate routine tasks, such as media monitoring and sentiment analysis, freeing up time for PR professionals to focus on more strategic initiatives.

3. Enhanced Analytics: With AI-powered analytics, PR professionals can analyse large amounts of data in real-time, providing them with actionable insights that can inform decision-making and improve outcomes.

4. Better Campaign Optimization: Machine learning algorithms can continuously learn and adjust their models, optimizing PR campaigns for better results.

5. However, it is important to note that while AI can bring significant benefits, it is not a silver bullet. The human touch and creative thinking will still be essential for effective PR strategies and tactics. PR professionals need to be aware of the limitations of AI and ensure that it is used in an ethical and responsible manner.

Me: How exactly ChatGPT can help PR professionals in their everyday life?

ChatGPT:
1. Content Generation: ChatGPT can assist with the creation of compelling and engaging content for PR campaigns and initiatives.
2. Media Monitoring: ChatGPT can provide real-time analysis of media mentions, tracking brand reputation and sentiment, and providing insights into consumer behaviour.
3. Data Insights: ChatGPT can assist in the analysis of large data sets to gain valuable insights into consumer behaviour, market trends, and campaign performance.
4. Report Generation: ChatGPT can automate the creation of reports, freeing up time for PR professionals to focus on other tasks.
5. Customer Service: ChatGPT can provide 24/7 support for customers, allowing PR professionals to focus on more strategic initiatives.

However, it is important to note that while ChatGPT can be a valuable tool for PR professionals, it is not a replacement for human expertise and creativity. PR professionals should use ChatGPT as an aid, not a substitute, and should always consider the ethics and responsibilities associated with using AI technology.

This interview was written within one minute. So it saves time a lot. Result is very interesting, as it says pretty similar things, which are in this book, but rather unexciting to read. It lacks that human touch which makes writing engaging. This means we, as PR professionals will not lose our jobs for quite some time.

Another practical skill of AI is verifying or drilling down on information. One of the first companies to combine journalistic skills with AI is Storyful. Their service is used by global media houses to verify media content and context. The Storyful team monitors key world events and verifies, for example, whether tweets depicting bombings in Syria, terrorist attacks or conflicts in disputed territories are true. For a change, Google is trying to use AI in an activity that most of us dread for obvious reasons: moderating discussions under articles. Its Perspective API analyses the impact of comments on the entire discussion and tries to detect toxic posts that may negatively influence the debate.

'Human as a Service'

Where we as leaders should definitely not fall short, is in the *use of modern technology, software and apps for campaign management and reporting*. Gone are the days of Excel spreadsheets into which we entered contacts of journalists. Tools such as Prowly and Cision can facilitate complete campaign management and media relations management, including reporting, and greatly increase the efficiency of PR professionals. Along with this, the demands of journalists are naturally increasing. In 20 years, the main content of a press release will no longer be just a few paragraphs of text – instead, journalists will have entire 'media rooms' where they can find all the written information and multimedia in one place, including archives. These are already available on the platforms mentioned, but only a few PR managers use them.

Technology will also inevitably impact team management, HR and internal communications. One example is Haiilo, an app that helps organizations increase team conversations and avoid communication and information barriers. In addition, the tool makes it easier for employees to get involved in what's going on in the company and for their leaders to better understand the trends and dynamics of their own organization through employee surveys and polls. The application also facilitates the measurement and evaluation of internal communication and, last but not least, helps with the implementation of diversity, equity and inclusion (see Chapter 7).

The change will affect everyone. For example, machine learning will speak to the delivery of commercial messages. Untargeted communication belongs to the past. Instead, every Internet user will – if they want to – get content that matches their preferences.

The work of the PR professional will therefore evolve dramatically. New positions will be needed, such as teacher and manager of robots or designer of artificial personalities. PR agencies will operate in a similar way to how, for example, software developers operate today – on the principle of so-called body shops. They will rent out their people to other firms for a certain period of time to set up their data processes.

Considering the above, it almost begs the question whether there is anything that AI can't do. The answer is (so far) unambiguous. Despite how gracefully AI has invaded our daily functioning, the dystopian notions that it will take away our jobs, relationships, and ultimately our freedom have not come true. It is still us humans who must teach AI the ways of journalism. And it will probably stay that way. As humans, we will continue to monopolize creative, intuitive, and authentic activities and social contact. The principle of communication will be 'human as a service'. After all, it is not in our interest to change anything in this regard.

*****

SARA POLAK

Welcome to the Cloud Civilization

We're not missing anything. We have the internet, home heating, and shopping at the click of a finger, a regular dose of dopamine (okay, frustration too) from social media, and more or less endless services. It's just that despite all the 'luxuries' we enjoy, at least in our Euro-American bubble, our society is cranky.

Why? In my opinion, as individuals, we don't realize our capabilities and power. After all, we can live with multiple identities, we are not beholden to the nation-state, and in many ways we have choices. I don't mean the illusion of choice in elections, I mean the actual choice of a life strategy that will ensure our safest and most optimal survival in the modern jungle.

*I can offer three steps to help us move nimbly through evolution and secure our place in the world. **None of us, after all, wants our only legacy to be a right-hand shake at the end of a 30-year career in one job and then living in suboptimal health, with a mediocre pension or no pension at all, and unfulfilled dreams.***

1. *To realize that our system is not built to understand, let alone value, individuals.*

2. *To acknowledge that the system we live in is not the pinnacle of civilization, but one of many (somewhat artificial) ways to organize society.*

3. *To embrace the concept of parallel cloud civilizations that we live in and have always lived in – we just used analogue technology to do it.*

Let's elaborate on each point.

Is our system built around the individual? Michael Collier wrote a great book, An Individual History, which describes how the fears, hopes, loves, disappointments and other emotions of an individual can, like the butterfly effect, affect the world around us and indeed the entire course of history. Unfortunately, our science cannot work with this concept. Unless we are talking about rare artistic geniuses such as Mozart, it is very difficult to work out in retrospect to what extent an individual has influenced history. It is also no coincidence that many popes and political leaders in the past have purposefully confused individualism with selfishness or outright Satanism. The system naturally dislikes individual thinking because it is difficult to predict, impossible to prepare for, and thus can undermine the system.

We must remember that the lowest common divider is indeed the individual and that nothing is self-evident. Even something as seemingly obvious as that every civilization must logically have writing (the Incas did not). For only then do we discover that the reality we live in is only one of the possible ones, and that all we know of the past and present is mere interpretation. Context is everything.

Here I would seamlessly pick up the second step. We tend to believe that our system is the best thing in the world. Yes, we have the relative luxuries of life, but that doesn't mean we have arrived at some philosophical ideal. The fact that the Roman Empire is taught in school rather than ancient China, the steppe peoples of Mongolia or the tribal system in Australia, coupled with the fact that we are touting democracy as the ultimate system without being able to see its flies, can be very dangerous.

There are many possible systems. Not just at the structural level (empire, kingdom, autocracy, decentralised organisation, republic etc.) but also at the scale level (family, team, ethnicity, intruder, household, neighbours etc.) Without realising it, we are living in about 10 parallel systems at once – this includes our work, friends, state, social media community, family... In the modern world, where we can be administratively 'hooked' in several countries thanks to country hacking, or even live in technological entities that are outside of state structures (such as cryptocurrencies or blockchain), it is no longer true that citizenship equals identity.

Suddenly, existence outside the state is starting to take on real contours. After all, parallel communities like the Roman catacombs, the resistance during World War II, or the Jewish communities in Rudolf II's Prague have always existed. But now they may simply have their own currency, exchange system, value ladder, technological infrastructure, and who knows, in time perhaps even a completely separate nationality. Or these communities may abandon the nation-state concept altogether and subscribe to global citizenship.

This brings me to the third part of the essay – the concept of parallel communities. Parallel Polis, the non-profit organization to which I belong, was founded on the visions of Václav Benda. He argued that replacing the existing system is often impossible and undesirable. It is therefore necessary to create a functional parallel system that takes the place of the 'official' one and offers people a real and safe alternative. It's a great thesis, and Benda is by no means the first to think of it.

The anthropologist Levi-Strauss writes about the binarity of the human brain – if we invent black, we must have white to go with it. This mode of evolutionary survival manifests itself all around us, just by the way we have grasped computers and the binarity of zeros and ones. For the sake of physics, we may not have much else to do, but it will be interesting to see how science gets shuffled by the kind of quantum physics that says two states can exist at once. Yet, from the point of view of history and sociology, we have always experienced two states at once (or even 30 states at once) in the structure of society, and quite naturally. This is the phenomenon of 'imagined communities' that anthropologists have been waxing poetic about for decades. They just didn't have the internet to easily prove their existence on a daily basis.

We can call this a social quantum phenomenon or quantum society – I call it cloud civilization. We live in parallel technological worlds that neatly intertwine with the physical one, and we do many if not most of our actions through them: buying food, storing money, international business, exchanging ideas, education. It is only a matter of time before nation states can no longer withstand this technological evolutionary pressure.

What's next? I don't want the state to fall. However, it is important to realise that nation states are a relic. Yes, they can work in some ways, but they need parallel pressure and competition to keep them from resting on their laurels. This pressure can (and already is) coming at a global level from cloud civilisations that exist, just not properly named and holistically explored.

Indeed, we have been living in cloud parallel civilizations for a long time. Information transfer is being democratised. We are no longer dependent on limited sources such as the state media or the local parish priest. We are in the best information situation we have ever been in. The democratisation of internet connectivity through projects like Starlink will further reinforce this principle. When we embrace our historic role as individuals and realize that we have the tools to change the world from our living rooms, our agitation will surely diminish a bit.

To be successful in parallel cloud civilizations, we need to master the basic tools of survival, just as we did millions of years ago. These no longer include flint, but the principles of data processing, under-standing our digital footprint and the principles of AI, or the ability to trade crypto and move on the blockchain. In short, to be that lifelong technology scout.

Taking care of ourselves and our survival is the best thing we can do for the future and society. Being an individual and a conscious 'citizen of the earth' are not mutually exclusive. Welcome to the cloud civilization – if you want to.

* * * * *

> *When we embrace our historic role as individuals and realize that we have the tools to change the world from our living rooms, our agitation will surely diminish a bit.*

Who Is Sara Polak

Sara Polak studied archae-ology and evolutionary anthropology at Oxford, but over time her attention turned to technology. She spent seven years working in startups in London and Los Angeles. She was awarded the Business Revolution Award from the UK Department for Interna-tional Trade, as part of the European Tech Women Awards. Forbes has included her in its 30 under 30 list. For the past few years, she has been back in the Czech Republic to spread awareness of artificial intelligence, break down technological prejudices and educate on the opportunities that technology brings to our society. She leads projects, organizes hackathons, works at Parallel Polis, collab-orates with CTU and is writing a book about memes.

Make Sure You Correctly Anticipate and Adapt to the Impact of Technology

Crypto. Blockchain. NFT. Concepts that belong to the future or other 'buzz words' that will lose their relevance after a while?

So-called *disruptive technologies*, which undoubtedly include all the above-mentioned terms, have been with us for decades, maybe even hundreds of years. These are technologies that will change the ways of society and send the future in a new direction. Nowadays, their onset (and therefore their subsequent impact) is faster than we are used to. Whereas the average lifespan of a company in the 1950s was more than 60 years, today it is under 20 years.[1] Research by Credit Suisse says that disruptive technologies are the reason. Nowadays, number of structural disruptive forces are at work and impact growth and profitability across many industries. In the words of Sara Polak: In the fast-paced evolution of today, only those who master the proper tools will survive.

It turns out that the key 'tool' for leaders is anticipation. Simon Sinek, in his book *The Infinite Game*, puts it perfectly when he says that the failure of companies is not due to technology per se, but to the inability of managers to adapt to the constant changes that development brings.

Don't Be the Next Kodak

Kodak is a prime example of how management myopia can lead a company into the abyss of history. This company, which needs no further introduction, had been in the limelight for decades thanks to the vision of its founder, George Eastman. In the late nineteenth century, Eastman managed to make photography – then an exclusive craft only practised by professionals – a pastime accessible to the masses. Over the following decades, Kodak came up with innovations such as the first commercially successful colour film, the circular slide projector, film for cameras... and finally the digital camera.

This was the moment when Kodak could secure its successful future for many years to come. However, the company's management

---

[1]Credit Suisse Equity Research (2017) *Global Equity Themes: Disruptive forces in Europe: A Primer*. Credit Suisse.

decided to suppress the disruptive digital technology – after all, they had built their business on classic analogue photography for years! The new technology would disrupt the company's existing business model. Kodak supressed digital photography.[2]

What followed was a gradual, subtle but clearly inevitable decline. Between 2005 and 2020, the company's revenues fell by around 91%. Today's Kodak is a shadow of its former leadership self. The reason? Kodak has abandoned the principle that brought it success: innovation.

Existential Flexibility as a Sign of Leaders

Disruptive technologies ask us to adapt – if we want to avoid the fate that Kodak suffered. Simon Sinek calls this need to respond to evolution an existential flexibility.

While existential shifts are not as critical in the communications and PR industry as they may be in other industries, they do come. Can you imagine if we still sent press releases by fax or mail? Technological changes are inevitably affecting our work too, and anyone who wants to be taken seriously as a PR professional must demonstrate their adaptability.

I expect that the biggest challenges for communicators in the coming years will be working with data, using the smart apps we discussed at the beginning of this chapter, and above all delivering campaigns that get results and have a clear impact on the organization – all while maintaining ethical standards, of course. This will not be an easy task.

The ability to see into the future and maintain existential flexibility will be critical to success. Leaders do not always have to take on this difficult task. As Sara Polak describes, the potential lies in individuals. Our challenge is to set up the system so that visionary talent can be heard. After all, Kodak's story would be very different if its leadership had listened to visionary individuals. One of them was Steven Sasson, the inventor of digital photography. He tried to persuade Kodak's management to put the inevitable existential shift ahead of short-term profits. Unsuccessfully.

---

[2]Sinek, S. (2020). The Infinite Game. Reed Business Education.

So, in the words of Sara Polak, let's be lifelong technology scouts. Or let us at least listen carefully to the 'scouts' amongst us. Especially when they tell us that an existential shift is coming – perhaps in the form of the rise of cloud civilizations. Not only will this increase our organization's potential to become a true leader, but it will also show that PR is an attractive field in which visionaries and innovators have a strong place.

ESSENTIAL STEPS HOW TO PREPARE FOR EXISTENTIAL SHIFT

1. *Recognize that Artificial intelligence (AI) and technology are making a significant impact in various areas of PR and communications.* Anticipate and prepare for this change. In 10 years you will probably be doing a different job. Or you'll be doing the current one very differently.

2. *Learn how to use artificial intelligence.* In the future, AI will perform predictive analysis of future end-user behaviour based on the content you publish. Its algorithms will take into account both implicit and explicit behaviours associated with any given topic.

3. *Prepare for how technology will change the job requirements of journalists and PR professionals.* AI or data analytics will bring new possibilities to journalism. Journalists will have more sources, data, and therefore more insider questions. PR professionals and leaders must prepare for these new dynamics.

4. *If you see your future in PR and communications, prepare for an existential shift.* It will require you to work with apps, artificial intelligence, data, advanced analytics, and above all, openness to innovation.

5. *Today's disruptive evolution requires you to master the relevant survival tools.* In our industry, this would be data processing tools, understanding your digital footprint, AI principles or the ability to trade cryptocurrencies or NFTs and use the blockchain.

9

WHICH PROCESSES WILL YOU NEED TO CHANGE OR ELIMINATE TO DELIVER MORE VALUE WITH LESS EFFORT?

The Role of Quality Management and Industry Standards

Public relations is a unique discipline. It combines high creativity with an emphasis on consistency, process and strict ethical standards. A good PR professional can deliver novel creative campaigns to his or her clients with the panache of an artist, while overseeing their measurable and effective execution with the precision of a mathematician. That's our job. But when it comes to our own companies and agencies, the bohemian approach often takes over. In that case, we carry the company's processes in our heads, assess client satisfaction based on lunchtime conversations, and choose tenders through a mixture of intuition and experience in a ratio that varies from case to case. Despite this, we know one thing for sure: Organizations that standardize their processes are more successful than those that don't. For this reason alone, the topic of quality management is worthy of attention.

* * * * *

WHAT WILL BE 'QUALITY COMMUNICATIONS' IN 20 YEARS?

Juergen Gangoly

For more than 20 years, I have been involved in the international PR and communications industry, working with colleagues from around the world to develop industry standards in areas such as ethics and quality. The invitation to contribute to this book nevertheless got me thinking for the first time, with a big leap into the future, about how standards and quality in communications work will probably be defined in 20 years' time.

Today, quality in communications agencies is defined, for example in the international Consultancy Management Standard (CMS), by the establishment and ongoing improvement of recurring processes and how these rules and standards are made transparently accessible to all employees. Today, the best communications agencies worldwide work according to the CMS. They strive for continuous improvement with regular CMS audits and ensure that they can offer their clients long-term reliability and the best quality. The CMS standard is constantly being further developed by the ICCO. At the moment, ICCO is discussing new chapters and agency standards in the areas of sustainability, diversity, and combating disinformation and fake news.

But where will quality management and industry standards be in 20 years? Will procedures and processes in companies for planning, developing and executing PR projects and campaigns still be validly defined by PR consultants, based on their individual life and professional experiences from the past? Or will PR consultants – or even former agency clients directly – simply consult machines with artificial intelligence? Machines that will then churn out how to achieve specific marketing and communications goals in the shortest amount of time, at the lowest cost, and with the greatest effectiveness with specific stakeholder groups?

Will PR agencies and consultants with integrity and ethics, with extensive personal experience, with knowledge of what can and cannot work in practice, with their abilities to evaluate and bring together complex social frameworks, perhaps not be needed in 20 years?

Will the simple input of a few initial factors, desires and goals into digitally networked 'PR robots' be enough to get a compelling story and the best possible approach to distributing the content suggested?

Will this robot content and the processes and actions associated with its dissemination even be monitored by qualified humans and evaluated in terms of social and environmental impact, quality and ethics? Will there also be independent audits and certifications for these 'PR robots'?

The question also remains, where will these originally stupid 'PR machines' get their initial inputs during their development? Who will set the standards and codes of ethics in what I see as the coming age of automated communications and automated relations? Will PR industry associations and international (human) experts continue to pay attention to do's and don'ts, or will communication tasks and final content decisions simply be handed over to machines with something like 'artificial intelligence'?

In my view, we should not and must not go that far. We must continue to put human intelligence and adaptability at the service of constructive – and above all peaceful – "human interactions" and public relations.

Humanity will not solve its communication problems in 20 years by 'PR programs' and computer networks understanding each other better and using common standards. It is imperative that we continue to take responsibility for content and 'human relations' ourselves – and, as current developments show, above all work again on common 'human standards'.

* * * * *

Will PR agencies and consultants with integrity and ethics, with extensive personal experience, with knowledge of what can and cannot work in practice, with their abilities to evaluate and bring together complex social frameworks, perhaps not be needed in 20 years?

Who is Juergen Gangoly

Juergen Gangoly is CEO and Partner of The Skills Group, one of Austria's leading communications agencies. Juergen has been working in the PR industry for over 25 years and served for over a decade as board member and vice president of the Austrian PR Association (PRVA) and Austria's PR Quality Trust Seal. He is  also a long-time member of the international board of ICCO and served as ICCO's European president from 2016 to 2020. As a co-founder of the international PR experts and quality audit network AgencyExperts.org, he coaches agency leaders and conducts quality certifications in the PR industry together with leading international PR experts. In 2020, Juergen was inducted by ICCO into the International PR Hall of Fame. His recent books and publications deal with Sustainability, Reputation Management and the Austrian Educational System, for which he developed a widely reported scientific system to measure the 'educational climate' in society.

MAKE SURE YOU FORMALIZE ALL YOUR PROCESSES

Common standards are the basis for successful cooperation – this applies not only to machines, but especially to people. As Jürgen Gangoly writes, the future shouldn't change that either.

PR is no exception. Here, too, quality management and the associated standards are an important indicator of how prepared an agency is for future cooperation. Quality standards for PR agencies have existed since 1997, when the CMS standards Jürgen Gangoly talks about in his article came into being. Their principles should be followed by all PR organizations that are serious about the quality of their work, especially when working with corporations and international clients. Because if a company hiring PR services follows standardized processes, it needs a communications partner – i.e. – an agency whose quality management can match those standards.

Leaving aside the world of public relations, it is safe to say that leadership in quality management means the ability to improve continuously. Leadership sets the mission of the organization and its future direction. As such, the responsibility of leaders lies in creating and maintaining the environment in which employees can fully participate in achieving the goals and objectives of the organization. Thus, good leadership is a driving force essential to improving quality because it sets goals and helps employees to realize those goals.

According to CMS, quality management is based on eight pillars that focus on all aspects of the organization, from leadership to people management. Let's take a closer look at these important areas which can deliver value to any organization.

Make your leadership communication the foundation for success

Not for nothing are leadership and communication the first areas of focus in the quality standards. The vision, values and purpose of the company are, in short, the foundation from which everything else is derived. The standards require an appropriate level of corporate governance, such as clearly defining objectives, but also internal or external risks that the organization might face. Assessing the sustainability of company practices is also an integral part of this.

Use business planning to create the roadmap to your destination

A business plan should be a realistic long-term programme that fits the market situation, the organization's potential and its future direction. But this is not enough: You must take care to ensure that such a plan is a true 'roadmap' and that management uses it systematically in managing the business and revises it when necessary. Of course, the company's business plan should be available to all team members.

When creating such a plan, you should be guided by the so-called SMART objectives. The term defines good goals as goals that are specific, measurable, achievable, relevant and time-bound.

Use your people to drive business improvement

The guiding principle of quality management is the pursuit of continuous improvement, so it is not surprising that this aspect is also among the areas of CMS evaluation. Organizations should strive to continuously improve their business, and use a variety of resources to do so. Ask yourself: Does our company involve employees at all levels in its development? Are we using employee input to develop innovative services? Do we have a system in place to collect, review and use key information to enhance management control and maximize business effectiveness?

Make your financial systems drive value not just activity

While the comprehensive financial audit is a separate area (and as such deserves a specific approach), the financial health of the business is also assessed as part of quality management. In this case, the standards focus on the principles of financial management control and the systems set up, such as the effective management of time reporting, invoicing and quotations, or an adequate financial reporting and capital control system. The key to future success is to ensure the financial systems in place focus on value creation not time utilization.

Ensure campaign management drives effectiveness

It is obviously essential to the quality of the work that the agency, or in house team, has a system to plan, manage and evaluate campaigns effectively. Essentially, this involves having procedures in place, such as campaign requirements and overall brief, subsequent campaign planning, follow-up and final evaluation. In addition, there should be continuous evaluation of the effectiveness of communication tactics. Campaign management also includes the identification and proper management of information, such as electronic and manual archiving or data handling and backup, retrieval, security, and disposal.

Use customer feedback to drive improvement and innovation

Client/customer satisfaction should be evaluated on a regular and consistent basis. It is only by methodically gauging customers' views that improvement in performance is possible. By listening to feedback, it will be possible to identify innovations that can achieve or reinforce leadership.

Use your purpose to select the customers to win

Every organization should have a system in place to attract the right customers, including managing enquiries and the overall process of selling. Such a system should be an integral part of the tools the organization uses. The specific configuration of such a system (i.e. a set of integrated marketing and sales activities) varies depending on the organization, its size, focus and also its purpose. By linking this to the purpose it is possible to make informed decisions about whom to sell to. A properly set up and followed system then brings brand awareness and, above all, new demand from potential customers.

Make sure you put your people first in securing your future leadership position

As Jürgen Gangoly writes, the experienced PR professional will continue to be a significant driver of business value in the future, despite the legions of algorithms that might dare to take over his/her job. PR and communications is, and will continue to be, a business of people for people. Moreover, teamwork, people support, workplace diversity and inclusiveness or corporate social responsibility are increasingly in the spotlight. The HR side of things thus plays a significant role in quality management. Every organization should have a clearly defined and universally understood system for the appraisal, training and career development of all its employees. In addition, the CMS Quality Audit gives special credit for the use of programs such as Investors in People. Receiving accreditation from this organization means that the company maintains high standards of care and development for its employees.

Ensure you have the capabilities and skills to succeed internationally

Does your company have multinational ambitions? If so, it should establish appropriate frameworks to ensure effective planning, management and evaluation of campaigns internationally. In such cases it is essential to have the skills, knowledge and understanding to run international campaigns.

Quality management is an often overlooked but very important part of any organization that aspires to be a leader. Don't underestimate it. The time invested will pay you back many times over. I dare say it is one of the activities that will make us 'less busy fools' as Richard Bagnall mentions in his prediction in his chapter on measuring PR.

Setting up processes will also help you maintain continuity and quality despite staff turnover. It will ensure that at any given moment, all team members know how your processes are working, what your company's goals are, and what strategies and tactics are leading up to them. And if they don't know, at least they'll be sure of where to find that information. Experienced consultants can help you achieve this desired state.

I first encountered the Consultancy Management Standard certification in 2007. Until then, I ran PRAM as an agency that concentrated on hiring great talent and took a very freewheeling approach to processes. What matters, after all, is the outcome, right? But when I looked into the principles of CMS, I saw an opportunity to not just become more effective but to be a leader in the Czech market.

How did it turn out? We have been able to improve our personnel management in the areas of onboarding and working with employees, whose development and education we now attend to much more systematically and effectively. Our client feedback proves that our clients are happier. We now conduct regular client feedback surveys using the Net Promoter Score metric. This allows us to make improvements where needed and to innovate our services to meet changing needs. As a result, not only do we have a world class Net Promoter Score, but we are now firmly among the top five agencies in the Czech Republic with a leading reputation for driving business momentum for our clients. We are also better able to work to use our Promoters' positive experience to present on the web, at workshops and to improve our overall reputation – thus attracting people and clients who believe what we believe and are seeking the value that we deliver.

The biggest step forward, thanks to adopting CMS has been in the area of new business. The system at that time (if you can call it that) was simply pursuing every enquiry that came our way. We had no set criteria for participation in tenders, nor did we keep statistics on what percentage of the pitches we managed to win. Thanks to CMS, we had to abandon this extremely inefficient method, which was akin to shooting in the dark. We used our purpose to guide us. We redefined who our target audience is, how we market to them, what we can offer them and what factors determine whether or not we can deliver the value a client is looking for.

Thanks to the implementation of CMS, we have reduced the number of pitches processed by an incredible 50%–70%, while the number of tenders won has remained identical. As a result, the effectiveness of our work has been transformed. The beneficiaries of

What Is Net Promoter Score?

Net Promoter Score (NPS) represents a measure of customer loyalty. It is determined by asking your customers a simple question: *'How likely are you to recommend our company to your friends or colleagues?'* Respondents then select values on a scale of 0–10, with zero representing the option 'not at all likely' and 10 representing 'extremely likely'. The resulting value is calculated by subtracting the percentage of Detractors (0–6) from the percentage of Promoters (9 and 10). Firms can thus achieve an NPS between −100 and +100. Generally, in the marketing and PR industry, achieving a value greater than +45 is considered an extraordinary result.

the time that is no longer wasted are our people and our clients – and ultimately the business.

Quality management will shake up your company. Only what is truly sustainable will remain. Things will change. We too have had to say goodbye to some clients where it was evident that the clearer definition of the value we can deliver did not match what they were looking for. Although saying goodbye was tough, both sides knew it was a decision that was in their best interests.

Anyone who wants to run a company efficiently and above all sustainably cannot do without quality management. Moreover, it is an integral part of ESG, which we discussed in Chapter 6, because it is the setting and standardization of processes that brings efficiency, resource savings and also equal access to all, based on transparent and clear rules, not on feelings and assumptions.

That is why, like Jürgen Gangoly, I believe that the future leaders in the field of communication and PR are the organizations that decide to follow the path of high quality management standards. CMS is one of those that holds enormous potential for leadership.

ESSENTIAL STEPS TO GET MORE VALUE FOR YOUR ORGANIZATION FROM COMMUNICATION

1. *Formalize and describe the company processes.* This will help you to run an efficient, effective and sustainable business.

2. *Review your processes regularly and communicate them internally.* Whether it is a business plan, strategy or HR principles, make sure these documents are up to date, reinforce your purpose and are known by everyone in the company.

3. *Reinvest the resources you save in new processes that underpin future leadership.* Such resources will find their useful application, for example, in ESG.

4. *Maintain ethical standards of work by describing processes to be followed.* By setting rules for your work, you raise the ethical bar for your employees, clients and the industry as a whole.

5. *Implement new technologies faster.* By following the company processes described above and investing in the personal development of your people, you will be able to incorporate new technology tools into your operations faster.

CONCLUSION: TRUE COMMUNICATIONS PROFESSIONALS WILL HELP PREPARE THEIR ORGANISATION TO LEAD IN THE FUTURE

What is public relations? What does it bring us? There are hundreds of definitions of public relations, but one caught my eye the most:

> *Public relations practice is the art and social science of analysing trends, predicting their consequences, counselling organisation leaders, and implementing planned programmes of action which will serve both the organisation's and the public interest.*[1]

This definition has a strong future orientation – the ability to predict consequences or outcomes. It also has a focus on serving the needs of both the organization and the public. That's what motivated me to write this book. Communications professionals have a unique opportunity to help their organization lead in the future by anticipating the challenges they will face and then helping to prepare the organization to master them.

Is the essence of PR really somewhere between science and art? I believe it is. A PR professional must have ideas, be able to captivate organizations and the public, and convince everyone that his or her client/organization and subject matter are worth engaging with. Being charismatic and understanding people – isn't that an art?

---

[1] World Assembly of Public Relations. (1978) '1978 Mexican Statement'.

A PR professional must also be a scientist, as there is also an analytical side to the work. Which aspect of a campaign, event or press release worked and which didn't? How to time the launch of communications and who are the stakeholders? How to link ESG and Diversity, Equity and Inclusion (DEI) to the purpose of the organization? What value has the campaign brought? Which applications and technologies will make us more effective? What campaign metrics to choose? This is not an art. It's a science, based on clear and verifiable facts. It requires data skills, patience and rigorous logical thinking.

The modern concept of PR appeals to the scientist and artist in us. This is what makes our field unique, incomparable and challenging at the same time. Contemporary public relations combines science, art and society into one interconnected territory that aims to deliver value not only to organizations, but also to the public, other stakeholders and the planet.

> *Contemporary public relations combines science, art and society into one interconnected territory that aims to deliver value not only to organizations, but also to the public, other stakeholders and the planet.*

To achieve this goal, we need to follow trends in our own industry and use modern approaches in all its areas – from quality management, ESG and company purpose, to crisis communications and campaign effectiveness measurement. This will require a lot from us: we will have to find not only the artist and scientist in us, but also, as Sara Polak says, the technology scout. We'll have to shed what's familiar and comfortable (goodbye, AVE) and learn a lot of new skills. A major part of this necessary existential turn will be rewarded for our work according to the value we deliver. Anyone who wants to succeed in the PR of the future cannot do without this ability.

If we can do that, I believe the future is exciting for everyone, and for those who choose career in PR, this is doubly true. Public relations is a modern and adaptive industry that is growing in importance. All kinds of personalities and talents will find their opportunity in it. Creative souls and analysts, writers and speakers, sociologists and data wizards, extroverts and introverts. For all of them, PR offers its wide arms and plenty of learning opportunities. There is perhaps only one type of person for whom our industry is not suited: those like the leaders at Kodak who hate change and believe in hanging on to the status quo. But people with that attitude will have a hard time in the future, whatever career they choose.

So, I'm blowing out the candle on my agency's 20th birthday and wishing that more and more diverse talent will choose to work in PR. As Michael Turney of Practising Public Relations says: 'The more sophisticated, more experienced, and more human its practitioners become, the more artistic, elegant, and effective its practice will be'.

APPENDICES

1. *Make sure you and your team are fluent in trends in PR and communication.*
   Why: PR evolves rapidly, and the future will bring a lot of changes.

2. *Organize a personal branding workshop with your leaders and start communicating their personal brand.*
   Why: Leaders will become more important for organizations.

3. *Support and collaborate with quality journalism, avoid disinformation and perform ethical PR practices.*
   Why: Media relations will remain crucial in the future.

4. *Start utilizing your created content across all available communication channels.*
   Why: It will help you leverage your work more effectively.

5. *At the beginning of every communications campaign, define the leadership value that the campaign will bring to the organization or client.*
   Why: Delivering value instead of effort will be essential in the future.

6. *Declare a clear purpose statement which incorporates the organization's values.*
   Why: You need to find your position in polarized society and show how your organization can benefit your stakeholders, including the planet.

7. *Make sure to cultivate inclusive people-first company culture in every aspect.*
   Why: Only then you will attract diverse talents which in turn will help you to attain leadership.

8. *Learn how to use technology practise PR more effectively.*
   Why: You will be prepared for an upcoming existential shift.

9. *Define all the changes you make and incorporate them into the com-*
   pany's processes.
   Why: It is the only way to make your company sustainable in the long
   term.

INDEX

9 781837 536337